Silas Casey

Infantry Tactics

For the Instruction, Exercise, and Manuvres of the Soldier, a Company, Line of Skirmishers, Battalion, Brigade - Vol. III

Silas Casey

Infantry Tactics
For the Instruction, Exercise, and Manuvres of the Soldier, a Company, Line of Skirmishers, Battalion, Brigade - Vol. III

ISBN/EAN: 9783337135133

Printed in Europe, USA, Canada, Australia, Japan

Cover: Foto ©ninafisch / pixelio.de

More available books at **www.hansebooks.com**

[BY AUTHORITY.]
INFANTRY TACTICS,

FOR THE

INSTRUCTION, EXERCISE, AND MANŒUVRES

OF

THE SOLDIER, A COMPANY, LINE OF SKIRMISHERS, BATTALION, BRIGADE,

OR

CORPS D'ARMÉE.

BY

BRIG.-GEN. SILAS CASEY,

U. S. ARMY.

Vol. III.

EVOLUTIONS OF A BRIGADE AND CORPS D'ARMÉE

NEW YORK:
D. VAN NOSTRAND, 192 BROADWAY.
1862.

ABBREVIATIONS.

S. S. Will stand for School of the Soldier.
S. C. " " " School of the Company.
S. B. " " " School of the Battalion.
E. B. " " " Evolutions of a Brigade.

Paragraphs marked 0 are suspended, and will not be taught.

CHANGE.

Paragraph 615, E. B., will be applicable to any skirmishers.

I C S.

E.

, brigade.

ehending
)vements
ngle bat-
lied to a

isting of
the rules
to two or

d in col-

reral bri-
e them-
the cen-

selves at
des, and
)8.

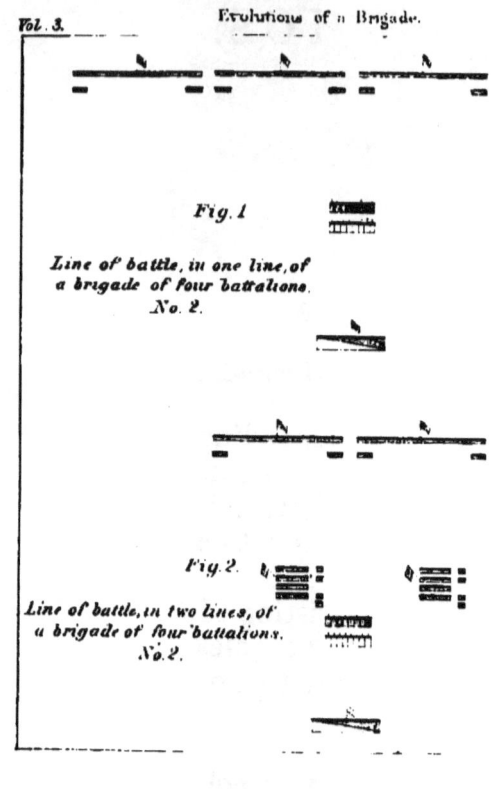

Fig. 1

Line of battle, in one line, of a brigade of four battalions.
No. 2.

Fig. 2.

Line of battle, in two lines, of a brigade of four battalions.
No. 2.

INFANTRY TACTICS.

TITLE VI.

EVOLUTIONS OF A BRIGADE.

General principles for the evolutions of a brigade.

1. The school of the battalion comprehending the principles and details of all the movements that ought in any case to be made by a single battalion, these principles will now be applied to a brigade.

2. In this instruction, a brigade consisting of four battalions will be supposed; but the rules herein prescribed are equally applicable to two or three battalions.

Posts of the brigadier-general in line and in column.

3. In line of battle composed of several brigades, the generals of brigade will place themselves at about seventy paces in rear of the centres of their brigades.

4. In column, they will hold themselves at about thirty paces outside of the guides, and abreast with the centres of their brigades.

5. If a brigade be acting by itself, its brigadier-general will, when it is in line of battle, take such position as he may judge necessary; and if it be in column, he will hold himself habitually at its head.

6. The brigadier-general will look to the exact and regular execution of all signals, notifications or commands coming from the major-general of the division to which he may belong; accordingly, he may repair, whenever he may judge his presence necessary, within the extent of his brigade.

General rules for commands.

7. The general (by which term, in these evolutions, will be understood the brigadier-general in command) will always give orders to his brigade by word of command.

8. When the general shall wish to cause a movement to be executed, he will give the general commands relative thereto. Each colonel will always successively repeat, with the greatest rapidity, on their reaching him, those general commands, unless the general has given, or sent to him, an order to the contrary.

9. The colonels having repeated the general commands, as just prescribed, will immediately command, and cause to be executed, without waiting for each other, the preparatory movements which, in their battalions, ought to precede the execution of the general movement.

10. The general will look to the prompt execution of these preparatory movements in his brigade, and rectify any error that may be committed by the colonels.

11. The final command, or that which determines the execution of the general movement, will always be given by the general.

12. The lieutenant-colonels and majors will repeat the general commands, whether of caution or of execution, as often as the wind or the noise of arms may prevent those commands from being easily heard from one battalion to another.

13. When, from any cause, a colonel shall not have heard the general command, he will, on seeing the battalion next to his own executing a movement, immediately cause his battalion to execute the same movement.

14. When a line has to execute a central movement, the general will go to the point which he may select for it, and give or send to each of the neighboring battalions, the order relative to the movement which each portion of the line has to execute, as hereinafter explained.

15. In column, commands will be extended, by repetition, according to the same principles.

16. When a brigade is formed in two lines, the second line, in all the manœuvres, will preserve its relative position to the first, and conform to its movements. The chiefs of the battalions of the second line are charged with the preservation of the proper distances. If the movement is to be executed by only one of the lines, the cautionary command by the general will be preceded by the words *first line,* or, *second line.*

Position of the brigade battery.

17. In line of battle, the brigade battery, consisting of eight pieces, four of them rifled, will be posted one hundred and fifty paces in rear of the centre of the brigade if it is in one line, and about thirty paces in rear of the second line if the brigade is drawn up in two lines.

18. In general, if exposed to the fire of the enemy, and circumstances do not require that it should join in the action, the battery can remove a greater distance to the rear than indicated above.

19. In all the evolutions, and without orders to the contrary, the battery will preserve its relative position, and conform to the movements of the other troops.

Position of the Cavalry of the brigade.

20. The cavalry of the brigade, consisting of four squadrons, containing about eight hundred troopers,* unless employed in a special manner, will be drawn up about three hundred paces in rear of the centre, or wings, of the first line, if the brigade is in one line, and one hundred and fifty paces in rear of the second, if the brigade is in two lines. In the evolutions, it will preserve its relative position.

---

* It is not intended, in the amount of artillery and cavalry here specified for a brigade, containing about four thousand infantry, to fix definitively the proportions which these arms of service should in all cases bear to each other. These proportions depend upon many exigencies, and are continually changing. As a general rule, however, the numbers here assumed are not far from correct, and will, at all events, serve to illustrate the manœuvres of these different arms in conjunction.

PART FIRST.

Article I.

To open and to close ranks.

21. The general, wishing to cause ranks to be opened, will command:

1. *Prepare to open ranks.*

22. This having been repeated, the lieutenant-colonels and senior majors will conform themselves to what is prescribed in the *S. B.*, No. 28; the colonels will immediately command: *To the rear, open order.* The general will then add:

2. MARCH.

23. At this, briskly repeated, ranks will be opened in conformity to what is prescribed in the *S. B.* Each battalion will execute the movement as if it were isolated; accordingly it need not be attempted to align the rear rank of one battalion on that of other battalions.

24. The general will cause ranks to be closed by the commands prescribed in the *S. B.*

Article II.

Manual of arms.

25. The manual of arms will never be executed in line.

Article III.

Loading at will and the firings.

26. In line, only loading *at will* will be executed.

27. The general, wishing to cause arms to be loaded, will command:

1. *Prepare to load.*

28. This having been repeated, the general will add:

2. *Load.*

29. This, immediately repeated, will be executed as prescribed in the *S. B.*

30. The general, wishing to cause the fire to be executed, will command:

1. *Fire by battalion* (or *rank*, or *wing*, or *company*).

31. This having been repeated, the general will add:

2. *Commence firing.*

32. The fire by battalion will commence with the odd-numbered battalions. The command *commence firing*, having been repeated by all the colonels, those of the odd battalions will immediately give the commands prescribed in the *S. B.*, for the execution of this particular fire.

33. The colonels of even-numbered battalions

will not give their first command until they see some pieces brought back to the shoulder in the odd battalion to their right; the colonels of the odd battalions, in their turn, will observe the same rule in respect to the even battalion, next to the left of each, and the fire will thus be continued by alternate battalions.

34. The fire by wing will be executed in each battalion, as prescribed in the *S. B.*; each colonel having repeated the command *commence firing*, will immediately give the commands indicated for the execution of this fire, without regulating himself by the next battalion.

35. The fire by company will be executed as prescribed in the *S. B.*

36. The fire by file will be executed in the following manner; the general will command:

1. *Fire by file.*

37. This having been repeated, each colonel will add: 1. *Battalion;* 2. READY. The general will then command:

2. *Commence firing.*

38. At this, repeated by the colonels, the fire by file will commence, and be executed as prescribed in the *S. B.*

39. The general will cause each of the foregoing fires to cease by a very short roll, or bugle sound, which will be repeated by the drums or bugles of each battalion the moment it is heard. As soon as each battalion reloads, its colonel will give the signal for the tap on the drum, or note on the bugle, for the return of the captains and covering sergeants to their places in line of battle.

40. The general, wishing to cause the fires to be executed by the rear rank, will command:

Face by the rear rank.

41. This having been repeated, the colonels will immediately add: 1. *Battalion;* 2. *About—* Face.

42. The general will then cause the several fires to be executed by the commands and means prescribed above.

43. The general having caused the firing by the rear rank to cease, and wishing to bring the line back to its proper front, will command:

Face by the front rank.

44. The colonels, having repeated this command, will each immediately add: 1. *Battalion;* 2. *About*—Face.

REMARKS ON FIRING.

45. In the presence of the enemy, the kind of fire will be determined by the character of the ground, and the state of the action.

46. A battalion, having in its front a height, or other obstacle to its fire, will advance as far as necessary, in order that its fire may be effectual.

47. Artillery having in general a greater range their infantry, should open its fire previous to the infantry battalions. The battery should protect the infantry while moving forward to attack with its fire a position in front; it should fire when the infantry advances, and withdraw when the latter commences the fire. The battery, in general, will not be moved in front of the troops, and without urgent necessity, it will not remain exposed to well sustained fire of the enemy's infantry. If so exposed, its fire will be rapid, so as to inflict as much loss as possible on the enemy.

To Rest.

48. The general, wishing to give relaxation to the line, will command:

1. *Prepare to rest.*

49. This having been repeated, the general will continue:

2. *Order*—Arms.

50. This having been repeated and executed, he will add:

3. *In place, rest* (or simply, *rest*).

51. This will be executed as prescribed in the S. B.

52. If, after arms are ordered, the general

wishes to cause arms to be stacked, he will command:

Stack arms.

53. This having been repeated, the colonels will cause the stacks to be formed; which being executed, each will immediately cause ranks to be broken, without regulating himself by any other colonel, in the manner prescribed in the *S. B.*

54. The general, wishing to terminate the relaxation, will cause a short roll or bugle sound to be given, which will be repeated by all the drums or bugles of the line, at the instant it is heard.

55. The roll or sound having ceased, the colonels will each command: BATTALION, at which the men will resume the fixed position of ordered arms; if arms be stacked, the colonels will cause the men to take arms before giving the command BATTALION.

56. The general will them command:

*Shoulder—*ARMS.

57. This having been repeated, the line will shoulder arms.

PART SECOND.

DIFFERENT MODES OF PASSING FROM THE ORDER IN BATTLE TO THE ORDER IN COLUMN.

Article I.

To break to the front, to the right or left into column.

58. The general wishing to cause the line to break by company or by division, will command:

1. *By company* (or *by division*) *right* (or *left*) *wheel.*

59. This having been repeated, the general will add:

2. March (or *double quick*—March.)

60. At this, briskly repeated, the line will break according to the principles given in the S. B. If the line is in march it will break as prescribed in the same school, and by the commands prescribed Nos. 58 and 59.

61. In that school it has been prescribed that, the companies having broken, the guides shall stand fast at the command *front*, given by their captains, although one or more may not be in the direction of the preceding guides; this rule will be observed from one battalion to another: thus, the leading guide of one battalion will not stir after the command *front* given by his captain, although he may not be in the direction of the guides of the preceding battalion; it is when the column shall be put in march, that the guides, who do not cover in file, will insensibly bring themselves on the direction so that each may march in the trace of the one next preceding him.

62. If it is the intention of the general, that the column formed either from a halt or march, should continue the march after wheeling, he will cause the colonels to be notified before the commencement of the movement, who will give orders accordingly.

63. The general, wishing to cause the line to break to the front, to the right, to march toward the left, will command:

1. *Break to the right to march to the left.*

64. This having been repeated, the colonel on the right will cause his battalion to commence the movement, which will be executed as prescribed in the *S. B.*

65. The following battalions will successively make the same movement; the colonels will seize the moment for causing their battalions to break, and each will be put in march, so that there may be, between its leading subdivision and the rearmost one of the preceding battalion, the distance of a subdivision, and twenty-two paces.

66. The general will cause the line to *break to the left, to march to the right*, according to the same principles.

REMARKS.

67. Whenever the brigade formed in two lines breaks or ploys into simple column for the purpose of marching, the colonels of the second line, unless ordered to the contrary, will form their battalions in the order indicated for those of the first line, and move them by the shortest route to their respective places in the brigade column, as soon as able to pass.

ARTICLE II.

To break to the rear by the right or left into column.

68. The general, wishing to cause the line to break to the rear into column by company, or by division, will command:

1. *By the right* (or *left*) *of companies* (or *divisions*) *to the rear, into column.*

69. The colonels, having repeated this command, will immediately add: *Battalion, right* (or *left*)—FACE.

70. The general will then command:

2. MARCH (or *double quick*—MARCH).

71. At this, briskly repeated, each battalion will break as prescribed in the *S. B.* If the line is in march, it will break as prescribed in the same school, and by the commands prescribed No. 68 and following.

Article III.

To ploy the line into close column, or in mass.

72. The general, wishing to ploy the line into column by division closed in mass, in rear of the first division of the first battalion, will command:

1. *Close column by division.* 2. *On the first division, first battalion, right in front.*

73. These commands having been repeated, each colonel will add: *battalion, right*—FACE, which will be executed by the designated or *directing* battalion, as prescribed in the *S. B.*, No. 160 and following; but in the others, all the divisions will face to the right, and the chief of the first division, in each of these battalions, will place himself by the side of his right guide.

74. These dispositions being made, the general will add:

3. MARCH (or *double quick*—MARCH).

75. At this, briskly repeated, the colonel of the first battalion will ploy it in rear of its first division, as indicated in the *S. B.*, No. 165 and following.

76. Each of the other colonels will, in like manner, ploy his battalion from a halt, in rear of its right division; but, pending the execution of the movement, this division will stand faced to the flank: the second and third divisions, each conducted by its chief, will be halted as it suc-

first division, third battalion

11. 19

column,
t guide;
d when
om the
ill com-
eft, and
he mo-
abreast

attalion
march,
oint of
st divis-
el, will
it; the
vement
it, and
es from
or four-
he first
o as to
leave a
etween
livision
ivisions
st, and
. The
guides
person,
self, in
ibed in

ttalion
in ad-

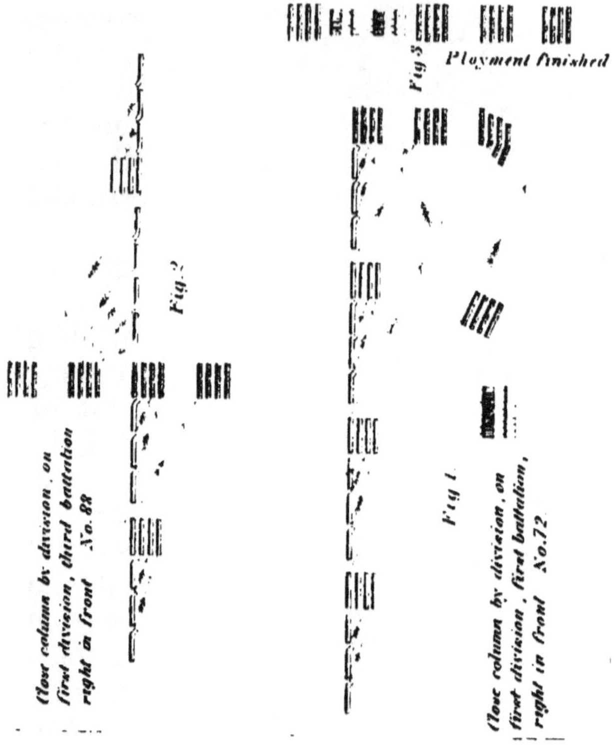

Vol. 3 Evolutions of a Brigade Pl. 2

Fig 3
Ployment finished

Fig. 2

Fig 1.

Close column by division, on
first division, third battalion
right in front   No. 88

Close column by division, on
first division, first battalion,
right in front   No. 72

cessively takes its place in the battalion column, the chief remaining by the side of his right guide; the fourth will enter in like manner, and when its head shall be at eight or ten paces from the right flank of the column, the colonel will command: 1. *Battalion, forward;* 2. *Guide left*, and 3. *March* (or *double quick—March*); at the moment the right guide of this division is abreast with the others.

77. At the command *march*, each battalion thus formed in mass will put itself in march, directing itself to the rear toward its point of entrance into the general column; its first division, conducted by the lieutenant-colonel, will take the shortest line toward that point; the other divisions will each conform its movement to that of the first, marching abreast with it, and preserving exactly the distance of six paces from one guide to the next; arrived at twelve or fourteen paces from the general column, the first division will incline a little to the left, so as to enter the column perpendicularly, and leave a distance equal to the front of a division between its guide and the rear rank of the last division of the preceding battalion; the other divisions will direct themselves parallelly to the first, and enter successively into the general column. The chiefs of division being up with the left guides of the column, will each halt in his own person, see his division file past, and conform himself, in halting and aligning it, to what is prescribed in the *S. B.*, Nos. 167-9.

78. The lieutenant-colonel of each battalion will detach himself thirty or forty paces in advance, to indicate the point of entrance into the column for his first division, and as each of his guides successively arrives, he will assure him on the direction.

79. The general, or officer charged with the execution of his orders, will place himself in front of the left guide of the directing division, to superintend the formation of the general column, and to see that the left guides accurately cover each other. *This rule is general for all ployments*, whatever the division on which they may be executed.

80. The line will be ployed in front by the same commands, substituting the indication *left* for *right* in front.

81. In this case the first battalion will execute the movement in the manner indicated in the *S. B.*, No. 178 and following.

82. The other battalions will each execute the movement in like manner, conforming itself to what follows: the first division, which will have faced to the right with the others, will remain by the flank whilst the battalion is ploying in front of it; the second and third, after having taken position in the battalion column, will be halted by their chiefs, who will remain by the sides of their right guides, and when the head of the fourth shall be at eight or ten paces from the right flank of the column, the colonel, observing the order of time indicated No. 76, will command: 1. *Battalion, forward;* 2. *Guide right;* 3. MARCH (or *double quick*—MARCH).

83. At the command *march*, each battalion, directing itself diagonally to the front, instead of to the rear, will be conducted and established in the general column, with slight variations, as prescribed No. 77; arrived at twelve or fourteen paces from the flank of that column, the head of the first division will incline to the right instead of the left, in order to enter perpendicularly, and to take its division distance; the other divisions will conform themselves to the movement of the first, and the chiefs of the whole will each conduct his division till its head is nearly up with the right guides of the general column; he will then halt his division, face it to the front, and align it by the right, its right guide having faced to the rear in placing himself on the direction.

84. The lieutenant-colonels will conform themselves to what is prescribed No. 78.

85. As each battalion takes its position in the column in front of the directing division, its colonel will command: *guides, about*—FACE.

86. To ploy the line in rear, or in front of the fourth (or last) division of the fourth battalion, the general will command:

1. *Close column by division.* 2. *On the fourth division, fourth battalion, left* (or *right*) *in front.* 3. MARCH (or *double quick*—MARCH).

87. These movements will be executed according to the principles given in the two preceding cases, but by inverse means: the fourth (or last) division of each subordinate battalion, being the first to take its position in the general column, it will be conducted by the lieutenant-colonel,

and the other divisions will regulate themselves by it.

88. If, instead of ploying the line on the first division, right battalion, or the last division of the left, as in all the preceding cases, the general wishes to execute the movement on the first or last division of any other battalion, he will command:

1. *Close column by division.* 2. *On the first* (or *fourth*) *division* (such) *battalion, right* (or *left*) *in front.* 3. MARCH (or *double quick*—MARCH).

89. Whether the right or left is to be in front, the designated or *directing* battalion will execute its movements as if it were alone.

90. If the right is to be in front, all the battalions in line to the right of the directing one will execute the movement as is indicated for ploying the line *to the front* on the left division, and the left battalions will execute the movement as is indicated for ploying *to the rear*, on the right division. If the left of the line is to be at the head of the column, the right battalions will conform themselves to what is prescribed for ploying the line *to the rear*, on the left division, and the other battalions to what is prescribed for ploying *to the front* on the right division.

91. If the directing battalion ploys on its first, or last division, the battalion contiguous to the directing division will execute its movement on this division: accordingly, the last or first division of the contiguous battalion, instead of re-

maining at a halt, will, at the commencement of the movement, file into the general column, at division distance in front or rear of the directing division.

92. If the line should be in march, and the general should wish to ploy, without halting, it will be executed according to the principles prescribed in the *S. B.*, observing what follows: As soon as each battalion has finished its ployment while marching, it will be faced by a flank, and conducted to its proper position in column.

REMARKS ON PLOYING A LINE INTO A COLUMN CLOSED IN MASS.

93. In the several ployments, the general will take, in preference, as the directing division, that of the right or left of the battalion, on which the movement is to be executed.

94. This method of ploying a line into column unites several advantages: *first*, it maintains, pending the execution of the movement, the battalions in all their strength, as each forms a separate mass; *second*, it occupies the least possible time, as each battalion moves over the shortest time to its place in the general column.

PART THIRD.

Article I.

To march in column at full distance.

95. The general wishing to put the column in

march, will indicate to the colonel of the leading battalion the direction to be taken by the headmost guide, and the colonel will immediately prescribe to this guide the means to be employed to assure the direction of the march, according to the principles established in the *S. B.*, Nos. 216–18.

96. These dispositions being made, the general will command:

1. *Column forward.*

.97. The colonels having repeated this command, will immediately add: *guide left*, if the right be in front, or *guide right*, if the left be in front.

98. The general will then add:

2. March (or *double quick*—March).

99. At this, repeated with the greatest rapidity, the column will put itself in march.

100. The guide of the leading subdivision will maintain himself on the direction which has been indicated to him, by the means prescribed in the *S. B.*, and the following guides will each march in the trace of the one who immediately precedes him, without regard to the general direction.

101. The lieutenant-colonel of the leading battalion will see that the headmost guide does not deviate from the directions he ought to pursue, and the same officer of each following battalion will also see that his leading guide preserves a distance equal to the front of his subdivision and

twenty-two paces, which ought to separate the battalions.

102. When a column has to prolong its march on a given line in order to form upon it *to the left* (or *right*) *into line of battle*, the general will always cause that line to be marked by one of the means prescribed in the *S. B.*, Nos. 228-30.

ARTICLE II.

Column in route.

103. The column being at a halt, if the general wish to put it in march in the route step, he will give the commands prescribed for the march in the cadenced step, with this difference—the command *march* will be preceded by that of *route step*, which will be repeated by the colonels.

104. The column being in march, the general, in order to cause it to pass from the cadenced to the route step, and the reverse, will give the commands prescribed in the *S. C.*, Nos. 315 and 317.

105. All the principles relative to columns in route having been developed in the schools of the company and battalion, it only remains to add here that, when a column of many battalions encounters a defile, which obliges it to diminish the front of subdivisions, this movement will only be made as each battalion successively arrives on the ground at which the preceding battalion had executed it.

106. Thus, for example, a column formed by company, encountering a defile which will only receive the front of a platoon, the colonel of the leading battalion will at once, or successively, according to the order of the general, diminish front by platoon: but the colonel of the next battalion will not repeat the commands of the preceding colonel until his battalion arrives at the same point, and so on of the others.

107. The chief of the column will take care to regulate the rate of the march according to the ground and other circumstances; he will always leave with the rear of the column an aide-de-camp to bring him prompt intelligence in case it find a difficulty in following.

REMARKS.

O–108. If the companies of skirmishers are in the column, the distances between the battalions will be estimated from those companies. Each battalion succeeding the first, will get its distance by stepping short; on resuming the cadenced step, these battalions will regain their distances by an increased pace.

Article III.

To change direction in column at full distance.

109. The general, wishing to cause the column to change direction, will dispatch an aide-de-camp to the point of change, and give notice of his purpose to the leading colonel a little before arriving at that point.

110. The change of direction will be executed

according to the principles prescribed in the *S. B.*, No. 273, and following.

111. Those rules will be observed in columns in manœuvre, although marching at the moment in the route step.

Article IV.

To halt the column.

112. The general wishing to halt the column, will command:

1. *Column.*

113. This having been repeated, he will add:

2. *Halt.*

114. This will be repeated with the greatest rapidity.

115. The column being halted, if the general wish to form it to *the left* (or *right*) *into line of battle*, and the guides require to be assured on the direction, he will place himself fifteen or twenty paces in front of the head, facing to the rear toward the direction which he may wish to give to the guides, selecting in rear of the column the second point which determines that direction, and establishing on it, the leading guide; he will then command:

Guides, cover.

116. At this, repeated by the colonels, the

lieutenant-colonels and senior majors will promptly cause the guides who may not be on the direction, to cover each other accurately.

117. The subdivision guides being established on the direction, the colonels, without waiting for each other, will immediately command: *left* (or *right*)—DRESS.

118. At this, briskly repeated by the chiefs of subdivision, each subdivision will incline to its guide, and be promptly aligned. If the new direction be such that a subdivision find itself many paces from it, the chief of the subdivision will cause it to march by the flank.

REMARKS.

119. As indicated in the *S. B.*, No. 232, the subdivisions of a column will not maintain the full distance.

ARTICLE V.

To close the column to half distance, or in mass.

120. Whether the column be formed by company or by division, the distance between battalions, when the subdivisions are at half distance from each other or closed in mass, will be equal to the front of a subdivision.

1st. *To close the column on the leading company.*

121 A column by company, at full distance and right in front, being in march, when the general shall wish to close it to platoon distance, he will command:

1. *To half distance, close column.*

122. This having been repeated, the general will add:

2. MARCH (or *double quick—*MARCH).

123. At the command *march*, the headmost battalion will close up to platoon distance on its leading company, as prescribed in the *S. B.*, No. 295 and following.

124. The other battalions will continue to march; when the leading company of the second battalion is at company distance from the rearmost company of the first battalion, its captain will halt it and align it by the left; the other companies of this battalion will close up on the leading one, and the following battalions will conform themselves to what is just prescribed for the second.

125. The lieutenant-colonel of the first battalion will assure the positions of the guides as prescribed in the *S. B.*

126. The lieutenant-colonel of each following battalion will go in advance to the point at which his leading company ought to be halted, and he will assure the positions of the guides by placing himself in rear of each, as the companies are successively closed.

127. If the column, instead of being in march, be at a halt, the general will cause it to close by the same commands. At the word *march*, the leading subdivision will stand fast; all the others will put themselves in movement, and the battalions will close up as just prescribed for a column in march.

128. If the column be marching in double-quick time, it will close by the commands and means above indicated, and agreeably to the principles prescribed in the *S. B.*

2d. To close the column on the rearmost company.

129. The column being at a halt, the general, if he wish to close it to half distance on the rearmost company, will command:

1. *On* (such company) *fourth battalion*, **to half** *distance, close column.*

130. This having been repeated, each colonel will command: 1. *Battalion, about*—Face; 2. *Column, forward;* 3. *Guide right.*

131. At the first command of its colonel, the battalion will face about: each guide will remain abreast with the front rank, become the rear; the rearmost company of the fourth battalion will remain faced to the front.

132. At the third command, the captains of the fourth battalion will place themselves two paces outside of their guides; those of the other battalions will remain behind the centres of their companies.

133. The general will then add:

2. MARCH (or *double quick*—MARCH).

134. At the command *march*, the fourth battalion will close on its rearmost company as prescribed in the *S. B.*, No. 317 and following.

135. The other battalions will close on the fourth, and when the colonel of the third sees that the first company of the fourth battalion has only a few paces left to take, he will command: *Captains on the flank of the column.* At this, the captains of the third battalion will place themselves briskly outside of their guides. When the eighth company of this battalion is at the prescribed distance, its captain will halt it, face it to the front, and align it by the left, its guide remaining faced to the rear: the other companies will close upon this company, and the remaining battalions will each execute what is just prescribed for the third.

136. Each colonel will face his guides to the front as soon as all the companies of his battalion are aligned.

137. The lieutenant-colonel of the fourth battalion will assure the position of his guides, as indicated in the *S. B.*, No. 324; the lieutenant-colonels of the other battalions will conform themselves to what is prescribed No. 126.

138. If the column be in march, it will be closed by the commands and means above indicated, and agreeably to the principles prescribed in the *S. B.*

3d. To close the column on an interior battalion.

139. The general, wishing to close the column on the headmost company of an interior battalion, say the third, will command:

1. *On the first company, third battalion, to half distance, close column.*

140. This having been repeated, the colonel of each battalion in front of the third, will command: 1. *Battalion, about*—Face; 2. *Column, forward;* 3. *Guide right.* The general will then add:

2. March (or *double quick*—March).

141. At the command *march*, briskly repeated by all the colonels, the third battalion, and those in its rear, will close up as prescribed No. 123, and following, for the execution of the movement on the head of the column; the battalions in front of the third, will close as indicated No. 134 and following, for the execution of the movement on the rear of the column; the eighth company, second battalion, will close on the directing company, leaving the interval prescribed No. 120.

142. If the column be in march, the subdivision on which it is closed will halt at the command *march*, and the subdivisions in rear will close in the manner prescribed for closing on the head of the column, and the subdivisions in front, in the manner prescribed for closing on the rear of the column.

REMARKS.

143. A column by division will close to company distance by the same commands and means.

144. The column being at full or half distance, the general will cause it to close in mass by the same commands, substituting the indication *column, close in mass*, for that of *to half distance, close column*.

145. A column, left in front, will execute those several movements according to the same principles. If the column closes on any subdivision in rear of the battery, this latter, before the movement commences, and upon an intimation from the general, will leave the column, and following the movement upon the flank, will resume its place in the column, when the manœuvre is finished. The colonels of the battalions next the battery, will be careful to preserve the necessary interval, prescribed No. 216.

ARTICLE VI.

To march in column at half distance, or closed in mass.

146. A column at half distance or in mass, being at a halt, when the general shall wish to cause it to march, he will give the commands prescribed above for putting in march a column at full distance.

147. The means of direction indicated for a column at full distance will be the same for a column at half distance or in mass.

148. A column at half distance or in mass, being in march, the general will halt it by the same commands as if it were a column at full distance.

149. The column at half distance or in mass, being halted, if the general shall wish to give a general direction to the guides, he will conform to the means prescribed for a column at full distance.

Article VII.

To change direction in column at half distance.

150. A column at half distance, being in march, and having to change direction, will execute the movement as prescribed for a column at full distance, with the difference indicated in the *S. B.*, No. 343.

Article VIII.

To change direction in column closed in mass.

1st. In marching.

151. A column closed in mass, being in march, and having to change direction, the general will cause the point at which the change has to commence, to be marked, and just before arriving at the point will command:

Change direction to the right (or *left*).

152. This command having been repeated, the

g at
inge
B.,

vely
oint
nan-

the
rec-
for-
pre-

gen-
vith-
after
o be
ding

t has
e di-
ving
new
com-

lonel
gen-

Evolutions of a Brigade.

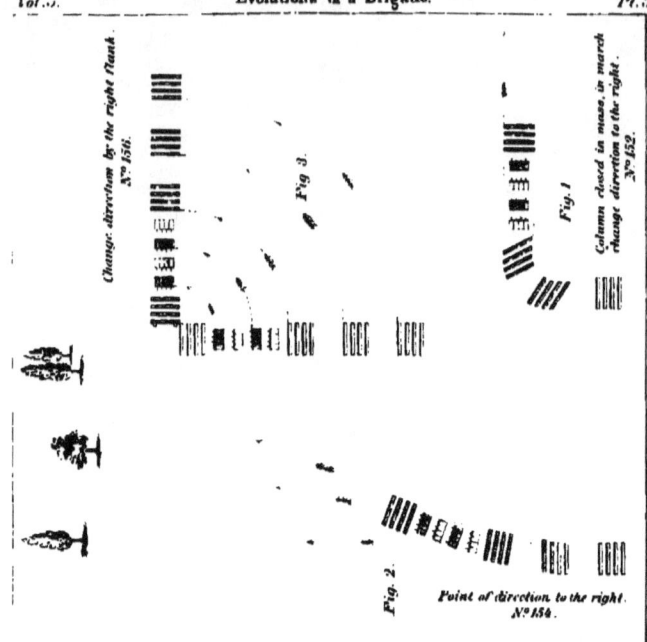

colonel of the first battalion will, on arriving at the point indicated, cause his battalion to change direction by the means prescribed in the *S. B.*, No. 345, and following.

153. The second battalion, and successively the others, will change direction at the point where the first changed, and in the same manner.

154. If, during the march of the column, the general should wish to give a new point of direction, too near the present one to require a formal change, it will be done by the means prescribed in the *S. B.*, No. 235.

2d. *To change direction from a halt.*

155. The column being halted, when the general shall wish to place it in a new direction, without any immediate intention of advancing after such change, he will cause this movement to be executed by the flanks of subdivisions according to the principles prescribed in the *S. B.*

156. It will be supposed that the column has the right in front, and that it has to change direction to the left: the general, after having caused two markers to be established on the new direction for the leading subdivision, will command:

1. *Change direction by the right flank.*

157. This having been repeated, each colonel will command: *battalion, right*—FACE. The general will then add:

2. *March* (or *double quick*—MARCH).

158. At this, the column will march by the right flank into the new direction in conformity with the principles prescribed in the *S. B.*, No. 367 and following.

159. The colonels will see, pending the execution of the movement, that the files do not open out, that the subdivisions enter in a square with the new direction, and that the prescribed distance between their battalions be exactly observed.

160. The lieutenant-colonel of the leading battalion will place himself some paces in front, and face to the guide of the first subdivision of the column, in order to assure the direction of the guides of his battalion; the lieutenant-colonel of each of the following battalions will place himself successively behind its left guides as they arrive on the new direction, to assure them in their positions.

161. A column in mass will change direction to the right by inverse means, and be conducted by the left flank into the new direction.

ARTICLE IX.

Being in column at half distance, or closed in mass, to take distances.

1st. To take distances by the head of the column.

162. A column by company being at half distance and at a halt, when the general shall wish it to take distances, he will indicate to the lieutenant-colonel of the leading battalion the point of direction in front, and then command:

By the head of column, take wheeling distance.

163. This having been repeated, the first battalion will take its distances by the means indicated in the *S. B.*, No. 387 and following.

164. Each of the other battalions will take its distances in like manner; but it will not commence its movement till the last subdivision of the battalion immediately preceding has left, besides the space equal to the front of a company, the distance of twenty-two paces.

165. If the column be in march, it will take distances according to the principles prescribed in the *S. B.*, and by the commands above indicated.

2d. To take distances on the rear of the column.

166. The column being at half distance, and at a halt, when the general shall wish it to take distances on the rearmost company, say the eighth company fourth battalion, he will first determine the direction of the line of battle, and direct two markers to be placed on this line as prescribed in the *S. B.*, No. 397. The markers being established, he will cause this line to be prolonged by one of the means indicated in the *S. B.*, No. 229 and following, and as soon as these dispositions are made, he will command:

1. *On the eighth company, fourth battalion, take wheeling distance.*

167. This having been repeated, the colonels will each command: 1. *Column, forward;* 2. *Guide left.*

168. At this, the captains of the fourth battalion will place themselves on the left flank of the column; those of the other battalions will remain before the centres of their companies.

169. The lieutenant-colonel and the senior major of the first battalion, will remain in their places in column; in the other battalions each lieutenant-colonel will place himself abreast with his rearmost company, and the senior majors each abreast with his first.

170. The general will then add:

  2. *March* (or *double quick*—March).

171. At this, the whole column, except the directing company, will step off: the lieutenant-colonel of the first battalion will take care to direct the leading guide a little within the line of battle.

172. The fourth battalion will take its distances as prescribed in the *S. B.*, No. 398 and following.

173. When the colonel of the third sees that only one company of the fourth remains to take its distance, he will command: *captains, on the flank of the column.*

174. At this, the captains will place themselves outside of their guides; the lieutenant-colonel will hasten to the point where his rearmost company ought to be halted, observing to take, between it and the first company of the fourth battalion, a distance equal to the front of a company and twenty-two paces.

175. When his rearmost company shall arrive abreast with the lieutenant-colonel, its captain will halt and align it by the left. The other companies of the third will take their distances as prescribed for those of the fourth battalion.

176. The remaining battalions will successively execute what has just been prescribed for the third. The lieutenant-colonel of the first will direct the march of its leading guide to the point where the rearmost company of this battalion ought to be halted, and then the senior major will replace him momentarily at the head of the column.

177. The colonels, lieutenant-colonels, and senior majors, will conform themselves to what is prescribed for each in the *S. B.*, Nos. 405–7.

3d. To take distances on the head of the column.

178. When the general shall wish to cause distances to be taken on the head of the column, say the first company, of the first battalion, he will direct two markers to be placed on the line of direction as prescribed in the *S. B.*, No. 408, and cause this line to be prolonged to the rear by the means indicated in the *S. B.*, No. 229 and following, these dispositions being made, he will command:

1. *On the first company, first battalion, take wheeling distance.*

179. This having been repeated, each colonel will command: 1. *Battalion, about*—FACE; 2. *Column, forward;* 3. *Guide right.*

180. At the third command, the captains of the first battalion will place themselves on the directing flank of the column; those of the other battalions will remain behind the centres of their companies.

181. The lieutenant-colonel of the fourth battalion will place himself abreast with his now leading company, and the senior major abreast with its rearmost one; in the other battalions the positions of the lieutenant-colonels and senior majors will be the reverse.

182. The general will then add:

2. MARCH (or *double quick*—MARCH).

183. At this, the whole column, except the directing company, which has not faced about, will step off; the lieutenant-colonel of the fourth battalion, placed by the side of the guide of its now leading company, will take care to direct this guide a little within the line of battle.

184. The first battalion will take its distances in the manner indicated in the *S. B.*, No. 409 and following.

·**185.** When the last company but one of the first battalion shall have taken its distance, the colonel of the second will command: *Captains, on the flank of the column;* at the same time, the lieutenant-colonel of this battalion will go to the point at which the first company ought to be halted.

186. This company having arrived abreast with the lieutenant-colonel, its captain will halt it, face it about, and align it by the left; the other companies of this battalion will 'take their distances as prescribed for those of the first battalion.

187. Each remaining battalion will conform itself to what has just been prescribed for the second. The lieutenant-colonel of the fourth will direct the march of its leading guide to the point at which its now rearmost company ought to be halted, when he will change place with the senior major.

188. The field officers will conform themselves to what is prescribed for each in the *S. B.*, No. 417.

    4th. To take distances on an interior battalion.

189. When the general shall wish to cause distances to be taken on an interior company of the column, say the first company of the third battalion, he will establish the direction in the manner indicated No. 178, and cause it to be prolonged to the front and rear; which being executed, he will command:

    1. *On the first company, third battalion, take wheeling distance.*

190. This having been repeated, the colonel of the third, and the colonel of the following battalion, will each command: 1. *Battalion, about*—FACE; 2. *Column, forward;* 3. *Guide right.* The colonels of the battalions in front of the third will each command: 1. *Column, forward;* 2. *Guide left.*

191. The general will then add:

2. MARCH (or *double quick*—MARCH).

192. The third and fourth battalions will execute their movement in the manner indicated No. 180 and following, for taking distances *on the head of the column;* the third will conform itself to what is prescribed, in that case, for the first battalion.

193. The first and second battalions will execute the movement as prescribed No. 168 and following, for taking distances *on the rear of the column.* At the commencement of the movement, the second battalion will put itself in march with the rest, and its rearmost company will be halted the moment there is between it and the first company of the third battalion, a distance equal to the front of a company, and twenty-two paces.

194. When distances are taken on an interior battalion of the column, the headmost or rearmost company of this battalion will be designated as the directing company.

195. A column in mass will take full distances by the commands and means just indicated. When it has to take half distances, the general will substitute in the first command, the indication *half* for that of *wheeling* distance.

196. All those movements will be executed according to the same principles in a column left in front.

197. In a column by division, distances will be taken according to the same principles as in a column by company.

REMARKS ON TAKING DISTANCES.

198. When the column takes wheeling distances on any of its subdivisions, or by the head of the column, the general will first direct the battery to leave the column, and will then close the interval which it occupied, by causing the three battalions which already have subdivision intervals between them, to close to subdivision distance upon the one which is isolated; or he will close this latter upon the others. He will then proceed to take wheeling distances, as prescribed No. 162 and following.

ARTICLE X.

Countermarch.

199. A column, right in front, being at full or half distance, when the general shall wish to cause it to execute the countermarch, he will command:

1. *Countermarch.*

200. This being repeated by all the colonels, each will immediately command: 1. *Battalion, right*—FACE; 2. *By file left.*

201. The general will then add:

2. MARCH (or *double quick*—MARCH).

202. At this, briskly repeated, all the subdivisions of the column will execute the countermarch, as prescribed in the *S. B.*

203. With the left in front, the countermarch will be executed according to the same principles.

Countermarch of a column closed in mass.

204. When a column in mass has to execute the countermarch, the general will command:

1. *Countermarch.*

205. This being briskly repeated by all the colonels, each will immediately command: 1. *Battalion, right and left*—FACE; 2. *By file, left and right.*

206. The general will then add:

2. MARCH (or *double quick*—MARCH).

207. At this, briskly repeated, the subdivisions will put themselves in movement, and the countermarch will be executed as prescribed in the *S. B.*, No. 426 and following.

ARTICLE XI.

Being in column by company, to form divisions.

208. The column being by company, right in front, and at a halt, when the general shall wish divisions to be formed, he will command:

1. *Form divisions.*

209. This being repeated by the colonels, each will immediately command: *left companies, left*—Face.

210. The general will then add:

2. March (or *double quick*—March).

211. At this, briskly repeated, the movement will be executed as prescribed in the *S. B.*

212. Each colonel will command: *guides*—Posts, as soon as the divisions of his battalion are formed.

213. If the left be in front, the general will give the same commands, and the colonels will conform themselves to what is prescribed in the *S. B.*, No. 455.

214. If the column is in march, divisions will be formed by the commands and means above indicated, and in conformity with the principles prescribed in the *S. B.*

REMARKS ON THE POSITION OF THE BATTERY IN THE COLUMN.

215. In marching in advance in the cadenced step, the battery of the brigade will take post directly in rear of its leading battalion. Marching in retreat, the battery will be posted directly in advance of its rearmost battalion. The pieces, in these cases, will in column, be formed four abreast.

216. Before putting a column, either by division, or company closed in mass, or at half distance, in march, the general, after giving the command, *column, forward*, will cause the leading, or three leading battalions, as the march is in advance, or retreat, to move forward, the distance of sixty, or one hundred paces, as the column may be by division, or company, in order that the battery may take its position in the column. The interval thus formed for the battery will be one hundred and forty paces.

217. In *marching*, in the route step, the battery will take post in rear of the column.

POSITION OF THE CAVALRY.

218. When in column, the cavalry will take such position either in front, flank, or rear, as the general may direct.

PART FOURTH.

DIFFERENT MODES OF PASSING FROM THE ORDER IN COLUMN TO ORDER IN BATTLE.

ARTICLE I.

Manner of determining the line of battle.

219. The different manners of determining the line of battle have been explained in the *S. B.*

Article II.

Mode of passing from column at full distance into line of battle.

To the left (or *right*) *into line of battle.*

220. The column being supposed to have the right in front, when the general shall wish to form it to the left into line, he will first assure the direction of the guides by one of the means prescribed No. 115, and following; which being executed, he will command:

1. *Left into line, wheel.*

221. This having been repeated by the colonels, the right guide of the company at the head of each battalion will place himself on the direction of the left guides, in conformity with what is prescribed in the *S. B.*, No. 465; the general will then add:

2. March (or *double quick*—March).

222. At this, briskly repeated, the column will form to the left into line of battle, and the moment it is formed the general will command:

3. *Guides*—Posts.

223. At this, the guides will take their places in line of battle.

224. A column, left in front, will form to the

right into line of battle according to the same principles.

By inversion, to the right (or left) into line of battle.

225. If circumstances require that a column, right in front, should form to the right into line of battle, the general, without occupying himself with rectifying the right guides of the column, will command:

1. *By inversion, right into line, wheel.*

226. At this, the lieutenant-colonel and the left guide of every company at the head of a battalion, will conform themselves to what is prescribed in the *S. B.*, No. 485.

227. The colonels having repeated the above command, will each immediately give this: *battalion, guide right;* the lieutenant-colonels and senior majors will rectify, with the utmost promptitude, the direction of the right guides of their respective battalions, without occupying themselves with the general direction of the column: and as soon as these dispositions are made, the general will add:

2. March (or *double quick*—March).

228. At this, briskly repeated, each battalion will wheel up into line in conformity to what is prescribed in the *S. B.*, No. 486.

229. The line being formed, the general will command:

3. *Guides*—Posts.

230. If, with the left in front, it be necessary to form the column to the left into line of battle, the movement will be executed according to the same principles.

231. If the general should desire to march forward without halting the line formed from the column on march, it will be executed in accordance with the commands and means prescribed in the *S. B.*

Successive Formations.

232. In the successive formations, the lieutenant-colonel of each subordinate battalion will always precede it on the line of battle, and establish a marker at the point where the right or left of his leading subdivision is to rest. He will take care to leave between this marker and the next battalion already established on the line, the interval of twenty-two paces, and then place a second marker on the line at a little less than subdivision distance from the first. The moment the lieutenant-colonel detaches himself, he will be replaced at the head of his column by the senior major.

233. As soon as the color subdivision of each battalion arrives on the line of battle, the color-bearer will step out and place himself opposite to his file on the alignment of the guides already established on that line, taking care to hold up his lance perpendicularly between his eyes.

234. As soon as there shall be two colors on the line of battle, the colonels will command: *guides*—Posts, after the last subdivision of their battalions is established on that line; but the color-bearers will remain in front until the entire line is formed. The general will then command: *colors*—Posts.

235. The lieutenant-colonels will assure with the utmost care the markers of their respective battalions on the line of battle, taking the colors as the basis of alignment as soon as there are two established on that line, and then assure with equal precision the direction of the following guides and color-bearer as they successively come on the line of battle.

236. Each colonel, after ordering in his guides, will cause his battalion to order arms.

Article III.

Different modes of passing from column at half distance into line of battle.

1. To the left (or right)
2. On the right (or left)
3. Forward by deployment
4. Face to the rear

} into line of battle.

1st. Column at half distance, to the left (or right), into line of battle.

237. A column at half distance having to form

to the left (or right) into line of battle, the general will first cause it to take distances on the subdivision he may choose to designate, by the means prescribed No. 162 and following; which being executed, he will form the column into line of battle as indicated No. 220 and following.

238. The general, when he judges it necessary, may order each battalion to form itself into line of battle as it shall successively have its distances, without waiting for the battalions engaged in the execution of this preliminary movement.

239. If the column be in march, and it be necessary to form rapidly into line of battle, the general will cause it to be executed by the commands, and according to the principles prescribed in the *S. B.*, No. 493 and following.

2d. Column at half distance, on the right (or on the left), into line of battle.

240. A column by company, right in front, being in march, when the general shall wish to form it on the right into line of battle, he will first determine the direction of that line, and then indicate to the lieutenant-colonel of the first battalion the point where the right is to rest; this officer will immediately detach himself with two markers, and establish them as indicated in the *S. B.*, No. 501.

241. If the direction of the line of battle be not parallel, or nearly so, to that of the column, the general, a little in advance, will take care to direct the march of the leading subdivision parallelly to that line, by the means indicated in the

S. B., No. 525, so that its guide, after turning to the right, may have at least ten paces to take in order to come upon it.

242. These dispositions being made, when the general shall wish the movement to commence, he will command:

On the right, into line.

243. This having been repeated by the colonels, each will add: *battalion, guide right.*

244. The leading subdivision having arrived opposite to the marker placed at the *point d'appui* will turn to the right, and the formation into line of battle will be executed as prescribed in the *S. B.*, 505 and following.

245. When the lieutenant-colonel of the second battalion sees the last subdivision of the first turn to the right, in order to move upon the line, he will detach himself with two markers, whom he will establish on the direction of the guides of the first battalion.

246. The leading subdivision of the second battalion having arrived opposite to the first marker, will turn to the right at the command of its captain, who will halt it three paces from the line of battle, and align it by the right against the two markers, placed in advance by the lieutenant-colonel.

247. The following battalions will execute their movement as just prescribed for the second.

248. The line being formed, the general will command:

Colors—Posts.

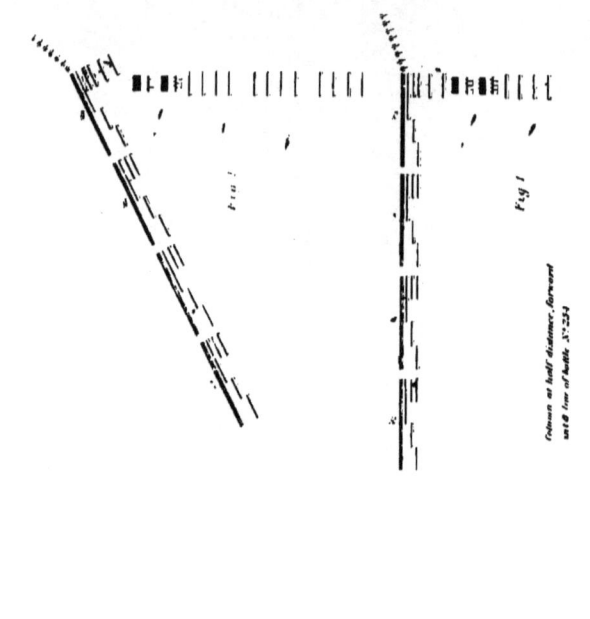

Fig 1

Fig 2

Colmun at half distance, forward
and line of battle N°234

249. At this, the color-bearers will return to their places in line of battle.

250. The general, placed at the *point d'appui*, will see that the colors of the two right battalions place themselves correctly on the direction which he may have determined for the line of battle.

251. The field officers will conform themselves, pending the formation into line of battle of their respective battalions, to what has been prescribed in the *S. B.*, Nos. 519–20.

252. A column, left in front, will be formed on the left, into line of battle, according to the same principles.

253. If the general should wish to commence firing pending the execution of the movement, he will give an order to that effect, and the several battalions will successively conform themselves to what is prescribed in the *S. B.*, No. 528. *This rule is general for all successive formations.*

3d. Column at half distance, forward into line of battle.

254. When a column at half distance, right in front, shall arrive behind the right of the line on which it has to form line of battle, the general will first determine the direction of that line, either at right angles, or oblique with the direction of the column; and then indicate to the lieutenant-colonel of the leading battalion the point at which the right ought to rest; this officer will immediately detach himself with two markers, and establish them on the direction indicated, as explained in the *S. B.*, No. 501.

5*

255. The head of the column having arrived at three paces from the line of battle, the general will halt the column, cause the colonel of the first to establish his battalion perpendicular to the line, if not already so, and then command:

1. *Forward into line.*

256. This having been repeated, the colonel of the first battalion will command: *column, close in mass;* the other colonels will each command: 1. *Battalion, guide right;* 2. *Head of column to the left.*

257. The general will then add:

2. MARCH (or *double quick*—MARCH).

258. At this, briskly repeated, the first battalion will close in mass, and then deploy on its first subdivision, by the means prescribed in the *S. B.*, No. 560 and following.

259. The remaining battalions will march in column, by battalion, toward the line of battle; to this end, the leading subdivision of each will break from the general column by a wheel to the left, and then direct itself diagonally forward, so as to arrive opposite to the *point d'appui* of its battalion, but distant from this point at least the depth of the battalion in column.

260. The head of each of these battalions, having arrived opposite its *point d'appui*, will turn to the right, in order to advance in a square with the line of battle, and when it shall be about three paces from that line, the colonel will close his column in mass, and deploy it on its first subdivision. If it is the wish of the general that the battalions shall remain in column, after arriving on the line, he will so direct the colonels.

261. The line being formed, the general will command:

Colors—Posts.

262. If the general should wish to form forward, into line without halting, he will cause the line to be marked in advance, and the movement will be executed according to the commands and means prescribed No. 255 and following, and the principles indicated *S. B.* Should he wish to continue the march without halting, the line will not be marked in advance, and the movement will be executed in conformity with the principles prescribed in the same school.

REMARKS ON FORMING FORWARD, INTO LINE OF BATTLE.

263. The precision of this movement depends on the diagonal direction taken by the battalions in passing from the general column toward the line of battle; the better to assure this direction, the general, colonels, and lieutenant-colonels will observe the following rules.

264. Before beginning the movement, the general will charge two aids-de-camp to determine the *points d'appui* on the line of battle for the right flanks of the different battalions, which will be executed as follows.

265. The first aid will gallop to battalion distance, and twenty-two paces from the general, placed at the *point d'appui*, and face to him; the general will, by signal of the sword, align him on the point of direction to the left. The second aid will gallop at the same time to a like distance behind the first, face to the right, and align himself on the first aid and the general.

266. The two aids being thus established on the line of battle, the general will cause the movement to commence; the second battalion will direct itself on the first aid, and the third on the second; when the lieutenant-colonel of the second battalion arrives on the line, the first aid will gallop to battalion distance, and twenty-two paces behind the second aid, and align himself on the latter, and the color to the right: the colonel of the fourth will immediately direct his battalion on this aid. Accordingly, it will be seen that the two aids will thus in turn place themselves one behind the other at battalion distance, and an interval of twenty-two paces, as soon as the lieutenant-colonel of the battalion, which directs itself on either, comes to replace him. The aids-de-camp will be careful to place themselves accurately on the line of battle, and at the true distance from each other.

267. From the commencement of the movement, the general, or the officer he may substitute, will place himself at the *point d'appui*, as in the formation on the right, into line of battle, and for the like purpose.

268. Every colonel will hold himself abreast with his leading company on the directing flank, pending the march of his battalion toward the

IV. 57

begins to
t is pre-

ach him-
-de-camp
his bat-
ty paces
large the
battalion,
. *B.*, No.

g behind
rward on
iples and

r, *into line*

, right in
ie line on
, the gen-
that line,
l of the
ii for its
tach him
em on the
he *S. B.*,

arrived at
rkers, the
the lead-
ed against

Vol. 1. Evolutions of a Brigade Pl. 5.

Column of batt.ⁿ distance, faced to the rear into line of battle.
N.º 271.

line of battle; and when the battalion begins to form, he will conform himself to what is prescribed in the *S. B.*, No. 590.

269. Each lieutenant-colonel will detach himself, in order to take the place of the aid-de-camp on the line of battle, when the head of his battalion is at about one hundred and forty paces from that line, and he will then discharge the functions, pending the formation of his battalion, which have been prescribed in the *S. B.*, No. 520.

270. A column, left in front, arriving behind the left of the line of battle, will form forward on that line, according to the same principles and by inverse means.

4th. Column at half distance faced to the rear, into line of battle.

271. When a column at half distance, right in front, arrives in front of the right of the line on which it has to form in order of battle, the general will first determine the direction of that line, and indicate to the lieutenant-colonel of the headmost battalion the *point d'appui* for its right; this officer will immediately detach himself with two markers, and establish them on the direction indicated, as explained in the *S. B.*, No. 501.

272. The head of the column having arrived at about company distance from the markers, the general will halt the column, and cause the leading subdivision to be marched and dressed against the markers, in the manner indicated in the *S. B.*, No. 532. He will then command:

1. *Into line, faced to the rear.*

273. This having been repeated, the colonel of the first will immediately command: *battalion, right*—FACE; the colonels of the following battalions will each command: 1. *Battalion, guide left;* 2. *Head of the column to the right.*

274. The general will then add:

2. *March* (or *double quick*—MARCH).

275. This being briskly repeated, the first battalion will form into line of battle, faced to the rear, as prescribed in the *S. B.*, No. 536 and following.

276. The remaining battalions will march in column, by battalion, toward the line of battle; to this end, the leading subdivision of each will break from the general column by a wheel to the right, and the battalion will then direct itself toward the line of battle, as in the formation *forward, into line.*

277. The head of each of these battalions having arrived opposite its *point d'appui*, will turn to the left, in order to advance in a square with the line of battle; and when at about company distance from that line, on which the lieutenant-colonel will have established two markers, as indicated No. 232, the colonel will halt his battalion, and cause it to form faced to the rear, into line of battle, by the means and commands prescribed in the *S. B.*, No. 531 and following.

278. The line being formed, the general will command :
3. *Colors*—Posts.

279. The general, colonels, and lieutenant-colonels, will conform themselves to what is prescribed No. 267 and following.

280. A column, left in front, arriving before the left of the line of battle, will be formed faced to the rear, into line of battle, according to the same principles and by inverse means.

281. If the general should wish to form into line faced to the rear, without halting, he will cause the line to be marked in advance, and the movement will be performed according to the commands and means prescribed No. 272 and following, and the principles indicated in the school of the battalion.

Article IV.

Column closed in mass, forward into line of battle, or into line faced to the rear.

282. A column closed in mass, will be formed forward into line, or into line faced to the rear, by the commands and means prescribed for a column at half distance, observing what follows. If the movement is forward into line, at the first command by the general, the colonel of the first battalion will command: *On the first* (or *last*) (subdivision) *deploy column;* the other colonels,

will each command: 1. *Guide, right* (or *left*).
2. *Battalion, left* (or *right*) *wheel.*

Article V.

Formations into line of battle, composed of two movements.

283. Habitually, and especially in the presence of the enemy, the formations will be made on the head of the column.

284. When, from peculiar circumstances, it is found necessary to form a column, which is at half distance, or closed in mass, right or left in front, either *faced to the front* or *rear* into line, on any battalion, other than that at the head of the column, the formation will be executed by the union of two movements, as will be explained.

285. In the first case, or faced to the front, the battalion on which the movement is made, and those in its rear, will form *forward into line of battle;* the other battalions will countermarch, and form *faced to the rear into line of battle.*

286. In the second case, the column having to form faced to the rear of the column, the battalion on which the movement is made, and those which follow, will form *faced to the rear into line of battle,* the other battalions will countermarch, and form *forward into line of battle.*

287. These movements will be executed by the commands and means already explained, observing what follows. The general, before commencing the movement, will cause the battalions in front of the line to be countermarched.

Article VI.

Columns closed in mass.

Deployment by battalion in mass.

288. The brigade column in mass, may be formed into line of battle by deployment: 1st. Faced to the front; 2d. Faced to the rear; 3d. Faced to the left; 4th. Faced to the right; 5th. Oblique to the front or rear.

1st. *Faced to the front.*

289. The general, wishing to deploy the column faced to the front, will first determine the direction of the line of battle, and cause it to be marked by one of the means already indicated, taking care, if the column be in march, to cause a mounted officer to be placed on that line, at the point where the head of the column ought to arrive.

290. If the column be at a halt, the general, before deploying it, will establish it perpendicularly to the line of battle, if it be not already so, by the means indicated No. 149, or No. 155 and following; if the column be in march, he will direct it on the point marked as above, but so that it may arrive perpendicularly to the line of battle, and he will halt it at three paces from that line.

291. The column being thus established, the general will cause it to deploy by battalion in mass, on whatever battalion he may choose to designate, say the first. He will place on the line of battle two markers, the first before the right, and the second before the left file of the headmost division, and then order a mounted officer to go beyond the point at which the left battalion will arrive, and to place himself exactly on the prolongation of the basis of the alignment.

292. These dispositions being made, the general will command:

1. *By battalion, in mass, in the first battalion, deploy column.*

293. This having been repeated, the colonel of the first battalion will caution it to stand fast. The colonel of the second will command: *Battalion, left—Face.* The other colonels will each command: 1. *Guide right.* 2. *Battalion, left wheel.*

294. The general will then add:

2. *March* (or *double quick*—MARCH).

295. At the command *march*, briskly repeated, the movement will commence; the colonel of the first will command: *right*—DRESS; at which the first division will dress up against the markers, and be aligned by the right. At the same time, the guides of the other divisions will cover each other accurately, each following guide taking the distance of six paces from the guide immediately preceding; the senior major will establish them promptly on the direction, and as soon as they are assured in their positions, each chief will align his division by the right. The chief of the first division, after having commanded *front*, in-

*By battalio,
on first batt.
column. N.º*

*Line of battl
battalion, by
mass on thir
deploy colur*

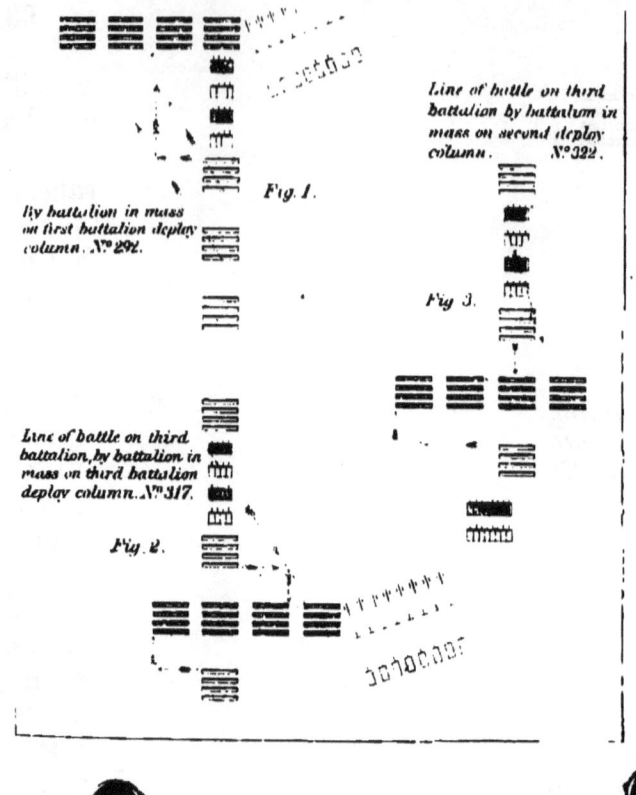

stead of placing himself before its centre, will remain on the right of the front rank, and the right guide will fall back to the rear rank.

296. The second battalion will march straightforward, and when it arrives opposite its place, it will be faced by the right flank, and moved on the line; the others will march in column by battalion, toward the line of battle, directing themselves as prescribed No. 259.

297. The instant the movement commences, the senior major of the second battalion will place himself twenty-two paces from the left flank of the column, to mark the point at which the battalion will face to the right in order to advance upon the line of battle.

298. The lieutenant-colonel of the second, at the commencement of the movement, and the lieutenant-colonels of the other battalions as indicated No. 269, will establish two markers on the line of battle, the right marker of each succeeding battalion, at twenty-two paces from the left of the preceding battalion.

299. After changing direction, for the purpose of marching in a square with the line, the right guide of the first division of each of the battalions, other than the first, will so direct himself, as to bring the right file opposite to the first marker, and when the head of the battalion is at three paces from the line of battle, the colonel will halt it, and command: *right*—Dress. At this command, each battalion will be aligned by the right, in the manner indicated for the first battalion.

300. The colonels will place themselves opposite the centre of the flanks of their battalions respectively, and on the side of the present guides.

301. The deployment being ended, the general will command:

    3. *Guides*—Posts.

302. At this, the markers, placed before the masses, will retire.

303. If the general should wish to form faced to the front into line without halting, he will cause the line to be marked in advance, and the movement will be executed according to the commands and means prescribed No. 292 and following, and by the principles indicated in the *S. B.* Should he wish to continue the march without halting, the line will not be marked in advance, and the movement will be executed in conformity with the principles prescribed in the same school.

304. If, instead of deploying the column on the first battalion, the general shall wish to deploy it on the fourth, he will begin by causing the dispositions prescribed, No. 289 and following, to be made, and then order a mounted officer to place himself on the line of battle a little beyond the point at which the right battalion will arrive; this officer will establish himself exactly on the prolongation of the markers placed before the head of the column.

305. The general will then command:

1. *By battalion in mass, on the fourth battalion, deploy columns.* 2. *March* (or *double quick—March*).

306. At the first command, the colonel of the fourth battalion will caution it to stand fast. The colonels of the first and second will each command: *Battalion, right—Face.* The colonel of the third will command: 1. *Guide left.* 2. *Battalion, right wheel.*

307. At the command *march*, the first three battalions will put themselves in movement; the first division of the first battalion, conducted by the lieutenant-colonel, will direct itself a little within the line of battle and parallelly to that line; the other battalions will execute their movements in conformity with the principles prescribed No. 296 and following.

308. The colonel of the fourth, seeing his battalion nearly unmasked, will command: 1. *Column forward.* 2. *Guide left.* 3. MARCH (or *double quick*—MARCH).

309. At the command *march*, which will be given the moment the battalion is unmasked, the colonel will conduct it toward the line of battle, and when at three paces from that line, he will halt it and align it by the left. The chief of the first division will then shift to the right as prescribed No. 295.

310. When the left file, first division, first battalion, is abreast with the marker, which has been placed by the lieutenant-colonel on the line, the colonel will command: 1. *Battalion.* 2. *Halt.* 3. *Front.* 4. *Left dress;* and the battalion will be dressed as prescribed No. 295.

311. The movement being ended, the general will command:

3. *Guides*—Posts.

312. Should the general wish to continue the march without halting, the line will not be marked in advance, and the movement will be executed in conformity with the principles prescribed in the *S. B.*

313. According to the same principles, the deployment may be made on an interior battalion of the column. The general, after having established two markers before the head of the column, will order two mounted officers to place themselves respectively a little beyond the points at which the right and left battalions will arrive.

314. These different movements will be executed according to the same principles in a column with the left in front.

315. In the preceding examples the line of battle has been established in front of the head of the column; the general may also establish it in front of any interior battalion, and then deploy the column on this battalion, or on any other that he may judge proper.

316. It will be supposed that the line of battle ought to be established in front of the third, and that it is intended to deploy on this battalion: the general will cause two markers to be placed before the first division of the designated battalion, and order two mounted officers to place themselves, respectively, a little beyond the points at which the right and left battalions will arrive; he will then command:

1. *Line of battle on the third battalion.*

317. This having been repeated, the first and second battalions, which are in front of the line of battle, will face by the rear rank; which being executed, the general will add:

2. *By battalion in mass, on the third battalion; deploy column.* 3. MARCH (or *double quick* —MARCH).

318. At the second command, the colonel of the third will caution his battalion to stand fast. The colonels of the second and fourth will each command: *Battalion left*—FACE. The colonel of the first will command: 1. *Guide right.* 2. *Battalion, left wheel.*

319. At the command *march*, the deployment will commence, the colonel of the third will align his battalion by the left. The other battalions will regulate themselves in conformity with the principles prescribed No. 295 and following. The markers, placed in the line by the lieutenant-colonels, to mark the places where the battalions which have faced by the rear rank are to cross the line of battle, will be a little more than a division distance apart, in order that the battalions can pass.

320. The battalions which have faced by the rear rank, will cross the line of battle between the markers, and when the first division of each battalion has passed the line three paces, the colonel, who will have remained in front of that line, will halt the battalion, and face it by the front rank; the two guides of the first division, and the covering sergeant of its left company, will place themselves on the line of battle, and will be assured in their positions by the lieutenant-colonel; which being executed, the colonel will cause the battalion to be aligned by the left.

321. The movement ended, the general will command:

4. *Guides*—Posts.

322. If, in establishing the line of battle on the third, the general shall wish to deploy the column on any other, say the second battalion, he will command:

1. *Line of battle on the third battalion.* 2. *By battalion in mass, on the second battalion, deploy column.* 3. March (or *double quick—March*).

323. This movement will be executed according to the principles just prescribed, but observing what follows.

324. The markers whom the general will cause to be established before the third battalion to serve as the basis of alignment, will be far enough apart to permit the battalion on which the deployment is made to pass between them.

325. At the first command the first and second battalions which are in advance of the line of battle, will face by the rear rank.

326. At the second command, the colonel of

stand fast.
will each
he colonel
right. 2.

ion is un-
 of battle,
hree paces
ilion, face
e left.
gained in
wo paces
econd, its
t, and es-

ployed as

to deploy
ause it to
ploy it by
or deploy-

it, having
o the left,
ving man-

o the line
imn, then

Evolutions of a Brigade.

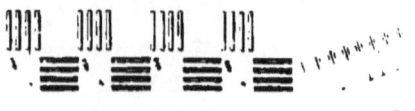

To deploy by battalion in mass faced to the left N.º 332.

Fig 1.

Deploy oblique to the front, line of battle on the first battalion, by battalion in mass on the fourth battalion, deploy column N.º 344

Fig 2

the second will caution his battalion to stand fast. The colonels of the third and fourth will each command: *Battalion, left*—FACE. The colonel of the first will command: 1. *Guide right.* 2. *Battalion, left wheel.*

327. As soon as the second battalion is unmasked, it will march; cross the line of battle, and when the first division has passed three paces beyond, the colonel will halt the battalion, face it by the front rank, and align it by the left.

328. When the third battalion has gained in marching by the flank, the twenty-two paces which ought to separate it from the second, its colonel will halt it, face it to the front, and establish it on the line of battle.

329. The other battalions will be deployed as in the preceding examples.

2d. *Faced to the rear.*

330. When the general shall wish to deploy the column faced to the rear, he will cause it to execute the countermarch, and then deploy it by the commands and means prescribed for deploying *faced to the front.*

3d. *Faced to the left.*

331. A closed column, right in front, having to deploy by battalion in mass, faced to the left, will execute the movement in the following manner:

332. The general will first determine the line of battle, on the right flank of the column, then cause the battery to leave the column, and the interval between the first and last three battalions to be closed up. He will then command:

1. *Deploy faced to the left.* 2. *By battalion in mass, change direction by the right flank.*

333. This having been repeated, each colonel will command: *Battalion, right*—FACE.
334. The general will then add:

3. MARCH (or *double quick*—MARCH).

335. At this, briskly repeated, each battalion will execute a change of direction as indicated in the *S. B.*, No. 365 and following, except that the chief of the first division of each battalion will place himself on the right of his division, after having aligned it.
336. The movement being ended, the general will command:

4. *Guides*—POSTS.

337. A column, left in front, will be deployed by battalion in mass, faced to the right, according to the same principles.

4*th. Faced to the right.*

338. A closed column, right in front, having to deploy by battalion in mass, faced to the right, it will change direction by the left flank, and then deploy by the means and commands above indicated; but as this movement is much longer than the preceding one, the general may, when circumstances require it, deploy the column by inversion, according to the principles prescribed for deploying faced to the left, observing what follows.

339. The general will first determine the line of battle on the left flank of the column, order out the battery, and close the intervals, as prescribed No. 332, and will then command:

1. *Deploy by inversion faced to the right.* 2. *By battalion in mass, change direction by the left flank.* 3. MARCH (or *double quick*—MARCH).

340. This movement will be executed according to the principles prescribed No. 335.

341. The deployment being ended, the general will add:

4. *Guides*—POSTS.

342. The battalions being thus placed by inversion, the masses will be deployed into line of battle in the direct order, when each battalion will be, in respect to the others, in the inverse, whilst its own subdivisions are in the direct order.

343. A closed column, left in front, will be deployed by inversion faced to the left, according to the same principles.

5th. *Oblique to the front or rear.*

344. If the column is so oblique to the line of

battle, as to require any considerable movement of the whole column, in order to establish a perpendicularity, the general will cause the line to be marked oblique to the column.

345. The deployments will be executed as prescribed No. 292 and following, observing what follows.

346. The battalions next to the one of formation will be governed in their movements by the direction of the line of battle.

REMARKS ON THE MOVEMENTS OF THE BATTALIONS OF THE SECOND LINE.

347. In taking wheeling distance preliminary to forming to the left or right into line of battle, in wheeling to the left or right into line, and in all the formations from column into line, if it is the intention of the general that the brigade shall be formed in two lines, he will, previously to the commencement of the movement, direct the colonels of the battalions constituting the second line, to move them out of the column, whence they will be marched to their proper positions in rear of the first line, under the direction of their chiefs.

REMARKS ON THE DISPOSITION OF THE BRIGADE BATTERY IN FORMATIONS FROM COLUMN INTO LINE.

348. In the successive formations from column into line, the brigade battery will generally take

earest the

olique fire
ilence the
g fire on

· a line of

ttalion in
advance,
ilion (the
e himself
direction
dicularity
ection, if

tion.

l of the
twenty-
s, face to
on their
imself in
osition of
ecessary,

Line of battalions in mass change direction to the right. N°. 368.

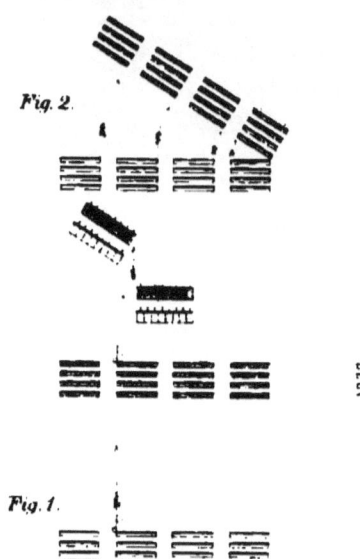

Fig. 2.

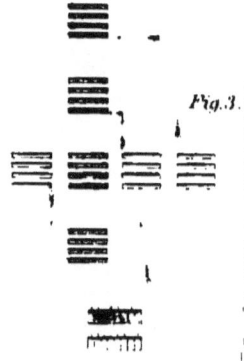

Fig. 3.

Fig. 1.

To advance in line of battalions in mass. N°. 351.

To ploy line of masses into column N°. 400

post on the flank of the brigade, and nearest the *point d'appui* of the formation.

349. It will endeavor to bring an oblique fire on the enemy, and will, if possible, silence the opposing artillery, before commencing fire on the infantry masses.

Movements which may be executed by a line of battalions in masses.

1st. The advance in line.

350. The line being deployed by battalion in mass, when the general shall wish it to advance, he will designate the directing battalion (the third will here be supposed) then place himself in front of this battalion, verifying the direction of its guides in respect to their perpendicularity to the line of battle, rectify the direction, if necessary, and command:

1. *The third the battalion of direction.*

351. At this, the lieutenant-colonel of the directing battalion will place himself twenty-five or thirty paces in front of the guides, face to them, and establish himself correctly on their prolongation; the general, placing himself in rear of those guides, will verify the position of the lieutenant-colonel, rectify it, if necessary, and then command:

2. *Battalions, forward.*

352. This having been repeated, the colonel of the directing battalion will command: *guide left*, and the other colonels, *guide left* (or *right*), according as they may find themselves to the right or left of the directing battalion.

353. At this command, the right general guide of the directing battalion will place himself six paces in front of his left guides; the lieutenant-colonel will establish him on the perpendicular, and as soon as assured in that position, he will take points on the ground in conformity with what is prescribed in the *S. B.*, No. 651.

354. The chief of the first division of the battalion to the left of the directing one will pass to the left of his division, taking post in the front rank, and the guide of that flank will fall back to the rear rank.

355. The lieutenant-colonel of every subordinate battalion will indicate to the guide of its headmost division the direction he ought to follow, and this guide will immediately take his points on the ground.

356. These dispositions being made, the general will add:

3. MARCH (or *double quick—*MARCH).

357. At this, briskly repeated, the line will put itself in movement; the general guide of the directing battalion will carefully conform himself to what is prescribed for the color-bearer in the *S. B.*, No. 659; the guide of its headmost division will march exactly in the trace of the general guide, preserving the original distance of six paces from him, but without constraining himself, in this, to minute exactness; the guides of the other battalions will direct themselves perpendicularly to the front.

353. The lieutenant-colonel of each battalion, being, pending the march, placed by the side of the guide of his first division, will take care to maintain between his battalion and that next to its right or left, on the side of the direction, the interval of twenty-two paces.

359. The chief of each first division will maintain himself exactly abreast with its guide on the opposite flank, and will superintend the march of the division, according to what is prescribed in the *S. B.*, No. 667 and following.

360. The other divisions will conform themselves to the rules for the march in column.

361. The colonels will hold themselves on the flanks of their respective battalions, each on the side of direction, and superintend the movement.

2d. To halt the line, marching in advance, and to align it.

362. The line being in march, when the general shall wish to halt it, he will command:

1. *Battalions.* 2. HALT.

363. The line being halted, if the general wish to give a general alignment, he will place two markers before the directing battalion, and then command:

1. *Guides on the line.*

364. At this, the lieutenant-colonel of each subordinate battalion will place two markers before its head on the alignment of those established by the general; and the chief of each first division will pass to the flank of his division on the side of the direction.

365. As soon as the markers are correctly established on the line of battle, the colonels, without regulating themselves on each other, will align their battalions by the flank of direction in the manner prescribed No. 295.

366. The battalions being aligned, the general will command:

2. *Guides*—Posts.

3d. The line marching in advance, to cause it to change direction.

367. The line being in march, it is supposed that the general wishes to cause it to change direction to the right; he will go to the point at which he may wish the right of the new line to rest, and place two markers, one at the *point d'appui*, the other at division distance from the first.

368. These dispositions being made, the general will command:

1. *Change direction to the right.*

369. This having been repeated, the colonel

of the first battalion will command: 1. *Guide left;* 2. *Battalion, right wheel;* at this command, the chief of the first division will place himself before the centre of his division.

370. The other colonels will each command: *guide right;* at this command, the chief of each first division will place himself before its centre.

371. The general will then add:

2. MARCH (or *double quick*—MARCH).

372. At the command *march*, briskly repeated, the first battalion will change direction by wheeling, according to the principle prescribed in the *S. B.*, No. 348 and following; its colonel will cause it to wheel until its front is parallel to the line of battle; he will then conduct it forward, halt it three paces from this line, and align it by the right.

373. The other battalions will be marched toward the line of battle, each executing in succession slight changes of direction to the right, so that, on arriving at twenty paces from that line, the headmost division may be parallel to it; to this end, the leading guide, advancing insensibly the left shoulder, will direct himself circularly to the right; the other guides will follow his movement in marching exactly in his trace, and the divisions will each conform itself to the movement of its guide as prescribed No. 154.

374. At the commencement of the movement, the lieutenant-colonel of the second battalion will place himself on the line of battle, and immediately establish a marker at twenty-two paces

7*

from the left flank of the first battalion, and another at division distance from the first, and at the instant of detaching himself, he will be replaced at the head of the column by its senior major.

375. The lieutenant-colonels of the other battalions will successively conform themselves to what has just been prescribed for the lieutenant-colonel of the second; each will precede his battalion, on the line of battle, by about fifty-five paces.

376. The movement ended, the general will add:

3. *Guides*—POSTS.

377. Changes of direction to the left will be executed according to the same principles and by inverse means.

REMARK.

378. It is essential that the battalion on which the movement is made should arrive perpendicularly to the line of battle; to this end, and conformably to the principle established in the *S. B.*, No. 352, the colonel of this battalion will cause the step of the pivot to be shortened, if this should become necessary; and if, notwithstanding this precaution, some of the divisions be not able to conform themselves exactly to the movement of the first, they will, on halting the battalion, be promptly conducted by the flank into the true direction before the battalion is aligned.

4th. *To march the line in retreat.*

379. The line being at halt, when the general shall wish it to march in retreat, he will command:

Face by the rear rank.

380. This having been repeated, the battalions will face in the manner indicated in the *S. B.*, No. 1223 and following; the chief of the fourth (or last) division of each battalion will place himself on the left of his division in the rear rank, now become the front rank, and the chief of each first division will place himself before its centre.

381. These dispositions being executed, the general will designate the directing battalion, and cause the direction to be traced as under the first head, *to advance in line*, No. 350, and then command:

1. *Battalions, forward.*

382. This having been repeated, the colonel of the directing battalion will command: *guide right*, and the other colonels, *guide left* (or *right*,) according as they may find themselves to the left or right of the directing battalion.

383. The general will then add:

2. MARCH (or *double quick*—MARCH).

384. The line will march in retreat according to the principles prescribed for marching in advance.

385. The line in march can be marched in retreat without halting by the commands and means indicated No. 380 and following, observing what follows. The command: *Right about* will be substituted for the command, *Face by the rear rank*, and the command: *Battalions forward* will be omitted.

386. The general having halted the line, and wishing to face it by the front rank, will command:

Face by the front rank.

387. This having been repeated, each battalion will face by the front rank; which being executed, the chief of the first division will retake his place in line, and the chief of the fourth his in column.

5th. To change direction of the line marching in retreat.

388. The line marching in retreat will change direction by the same means and commands as if it were advancing, observing what follows.

389. It is supposed that the general wishes to change direction to the left; he will place two markers on the new direction, the first at the *point d'appui*, and the second at such distance from the first that the battalion may easily pass between them.

390. The first battalion will be conducted to and established on the new direction as indicated Nos. 368 and 372; but it will cross the line of battle: and when the first division has passed three paces beyond, the colonel will halt the battalion, and face it by the front rank.

391. As soon as the battalion faces, the guides of the first division will place themselves on the line of battle, and be assured in their positions by the lieutenant-colonel; which being done, the colonel will align the battalion by the right.

392. The other colonels will each direct his battalion so that it may arrive when at twenty paces, parallelly to the line of battle; he will then cause it to pass that line, between the two markers placed in advance by the lieutenant-colonel in the manner indicated No. 389. When the first division has passed three paces beyond the line, the battalion will be halted, faced by the front rank, and aligned as prescribed for the first.

393. A line of battalion masses, left in front, will march and change direction, advancing and retreating, according to the same principles and inverse means; the fourth or last division of each mass will conform itself to what is prescribed for the first, and reciprocally.

6th. To break the line formed by battalion in mass, into column.

394. The line being at a halt, when the general shall wish to break it to the right into column by battalion, he will command:

1. *By battalion, right in front, into column.*

395. This having been repeated, the lieutenant-colonel of each battalion will place a marker before the left guide of its first division, and a second at division distance from the first in a direction perpendicular to the line of battle.

396. At the same time, each colonel will command: 1. *Change direction by the left flank;* 2. *Battalion, left*—FACE.

397. These dispositions being made, the general will add:

2. MARCH (or *double quick*—MARCH).

398. At this, each battalion will change direction by the means indicated in the *S. B.*

7th. To ploy the line of masses into column.

399. When a line of battalions in mass has to be ployed into column, as the battalions, by reason of their depth, and the smallness of the intervals between them, cannot be directed diagonally toward the points at which they ought respectively to enter the column, the movement will be executed in the following manner:

400. It will be supposed that the line ought to be ployed on the third battalion, right in front; the general will place himself in front of this battalion, and after assuring himself that the guides are correctly placed, he will command:

1. *By battalion in mass, on the third battalion, right in front, into column.* 2. MARCH (or *double quick*—MARCH).

401. At the first command, each colonel who

finds himself to the right of the directing battalion, will command: 1. *Column, forward.* 2. *Guide left.*

402. The colonel to the left of the directing battalion, will give the same commands after causing his battalion to face about.

403. At the command *march*, the movement will commence: the first and second battalions will march to the front, and when the last division of the second battalion shall have passed division distance, beyond the first division of the third, the colonel will cause his battalion to face to the left, in marching, in order to take its place in column; when the left guides arrive on the direction of those of the third, the colonel of the second will halt it, and cause it to face to the front.

404. At the moment of halting, the left guides, facing to the rear, will place themselves on the prolongation of those of the third battalion; and the lieutenant-colonel, placed in their rear, will assure them on the direction; which being done, the colonel will cause his battalion to be aligned by the left, and then order the guides to face about.

405. The colonel of the first battalion will conform himself to what has just been prescribed for the colonel of the second, as his last division has passed division distance beyond the front rank, first division, of the battalion which entered the column next before his own.

406. The fourth battalion will enter the column in like manner; the colonel of the fourth will cause it to face to the left in marching, when its first division has passed division distance beyond the rear rank, last division, of the third battalion, and he will halt his battalion when its left guides are on the direction of those of the third.

407. At the moment of halting, the guides of the fourth will promptly place themselves on the prolongation of those of the third battalion, and the lieutenant-colonel will assure them on that direction; which being done, the colonel will cause his battalion to be aligned by the left.

408. A line of masses will be ployed into column, left in front, according to the same principles and by inverse means.

409. If the line of battalions in mass are in march, the column can be formed either in rear of the first, or last battalion of the line, without halting, by the commands and means prescribed No. 399 and following; and by the principles indicated No. 199 and following, *S. B.*, observing what follows. The battalions to the right or left of the one of formation, will face by the left or right flank, instead of facing about, and each will take its place in column, as soon as able to pass.

REMARKS ON FORMING A COLUMN CLOSED IN MASS, FROM A LINE OF BATTALIONS IN MASS.

410. If it is found expedient to give a greater concentration to the troops, the general may form the whole column closed in mass, with a distance of but six paces between the division guides.

l by

eral
tal-
, he
t of
nce
he
the
91.
en-

on,
ble

the
the
m-
rd,
m-
ide

ed,
al-
he
st,
es
he
ie,
a
nt

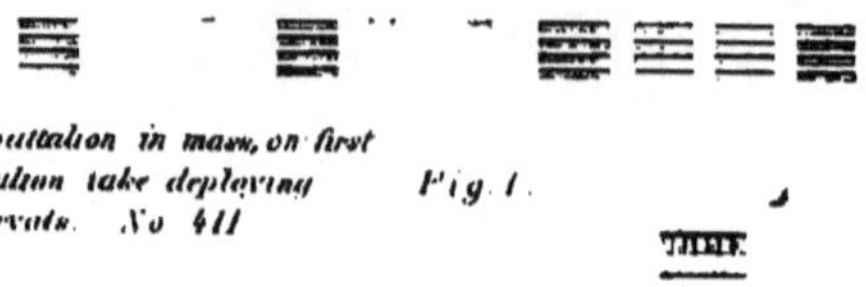

Evolutions of a Brigade   Pl. 9

By battalion in mass, on first battalion take deploying intervals. No. 411   Fig. 1.

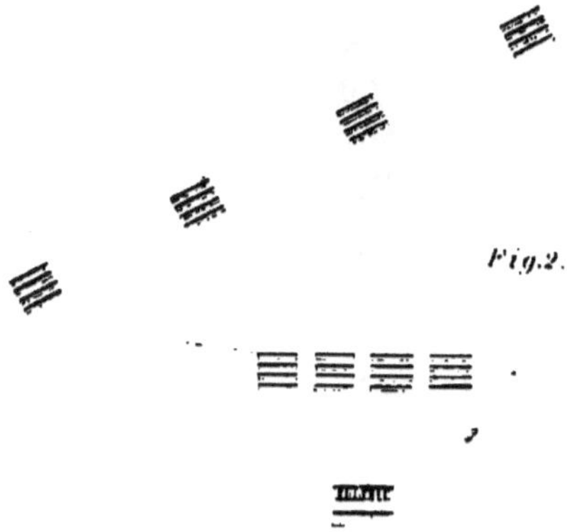

   Fig. 2.   *By battalion in mass, forward, on third battalion, take deploying intervals. No. 420.*

8th. To take deploying intervals from a line formed by battalions in mass.

411. The line being at a halt, when the general shall wish to take deploying intervals by battalion in mass, on any battalion, say the third, he will cause two markers to be placed in front of that battalion, a little less than division distance apart, and three paces in front of the line; he will then cause the line to be prolonged, to the right and left, by the means prescribed No. 291.

412. These dispositions being made, the general will command:

1. *By battalion in mass, on the third battalion, take deploying intervals.* 2. MARCH (or *double quick*—MARCH).

413. At the first command, the colonel of the third will caution his battalion to stand fast; the colonels of the first two battalions, will command: 1. *Right face;* 2. *Battalion forward, guide left.* The colonel of the fourth, will command: 1. *Left face;* 2. *Battalion forward, guide right.*

414. At the command *march,* briskly repeated, the colonel of the third will establish his battalion on the markers in front, dressing it to the left, in the manner prescribed No. 295; the first, second, and fourth battalions will put themselves in march by the flanks, and when each of the battalions on the right of the directing one, separates itself from the battalion on its left, a distance equal to twenty-two paces and the front of three divisions, its colonel will halt it, face it to the front, and dress it to the left upon the markers, which have been established by the lieutenant-colonel.

415. The colonel of the fourth, when he has separated his battalion a like distance from the third, will halt it, face it to the front, and dress it to the right upon the markers, as indicated above.

416. The lieutenant-colonels of the battalions, other than the third, will each establish for his battalion, two markers on the line of battle, in the manner indicated No. 269.

417. The movement being ended, the general will command:

3. *Guides*—Posts.

418. If, however, it should be the wish of the general to establish the battalions in mass, at deploying intervals, on a line of battle in front of the present one, either *parallel* or *oblique* to it, he will establish two markers to indicate where the battalion of direction, say the third, shall rest, and cause the line of battle to be marked, as prescribed No. 291.

420. These dispositions being made, the general will then command:

1. *By battalion in mass, forward, on the third battalion, take deploying intervals.* 2. March, (or *double quick*—March.)

421. At the first command, the colonels of the

different battalions, seeing the position of the markers of the directing battalion, will give such cautionary commands as shall be necessary, in order to direct their battalions toward their positions on the new line of battle.

422. At the command *march*, briskly repeated, the battalions will be put in march, and, conducted by their colonels, will be established in their proper posts on the new line of battle.

423. The lieutenant-colonels, as prescribed No. 269, will each precede his battalion upon the new line of battle, and establish markers to indicate where the head of his battalion shall rest.

424. The movement being ended, the general will command:

3. *Guides*—Posts.

REMARKS ON THE DISPOSITIONS OF THE COMPANIES OF SKIRMISHERS IN A LINE OF BATTALIONS IN MASS.

0-425. Whenever the battalions are formed by mass into line of battle, with an interval of twenty-two paces between them, the platoon columns of skirmishers of each battalion will take a position closed in mass in rear of its last division; the first platoon column, in rear of the outer platoon of the right company, and the second platoon column in rear of the outer platoon of the left company. In marching in advance, or retreat, or in changing direction, they will retain this position. On the formation of column, or when deploying intervals are taken, the skirmishers will resume their proper places, as prescribed in the *S. B.*

REMARKS ON INVERSIONS.

426. The principles prescribed in the *S. B.*, No. 642 and following, for *breaking* or *ploying* into column a single battalion, formed in line of battle by inversion, are applicable to a brigade, when formed in line by inversion in the manner indicated No. 226 and following; but when the battalions are placed, in respect to each other, in the inverse order, whilst their subdivisions are in the direct order, as indicated No. 342, other means, to be immediately prescribed, will be employed for breaking or ploying the line into column if it be desired to replace the battalions in the direct order. The principles prescribed in the *S. B.*, Nos. 639-41 are also applicable to a brigade.

427. It will be supposed that the general, in causing the line to break, wishes to march it to the left; he will order each colonel to cause his battalion to break to the right in order to march toward the left (in column at full distance) as if it were isolated; and as soon as the battalions break he will put them in march all at the same time: in this way the column will find itself united and formed in the direct order as soon as the last subdivision of each battalion has turned into the new direction.

428. If, instead of breaking the line (into column at full distance), the general shall wish to ploy it into column, say on the third battalion, so that the first battalion may be in front, he will order the colonel of the third to ploy it into column, right in front, on its second division; at the

to
ont,
ion,
mn
in
at-

to
be
the
me

to
ng
ay
he

el
ill
r-
ed

o,

To halt the line and to align it No. 463.

To advance in line of battle deployed. No. 430.

same time he will order the other colonels to ploy their respective battalions, right in front, on the division nearest to the directing battalion, and then cause the masses to enter the column as follows: the first and second battalions in front, and the fourth in rear of the directing battalion.

429. If in breaking the line, it be desired to march toward the right, or if, in ploying it, it be desired to place the fourth battalion in front, the movement will be executed according to the same principles and by inverse means.

PART FIFTH.

Article I.

To advance in line of battle deployed.

430. The general, wishing to cause the line to advance in this order, will choose as the directing battalion, say the third, the one which he may deem most favorably placed for the purpose; he will approach this battalion and command:

1. *The third the battalion of direction.*

431. This having been repeated, the colonel and lieutenant-colonel of every battalion will place themselves in rear and in front of the color-file of their respective battalions, as prescribed in the *S. B.*, Nos. 648–9.

432. The colonel of the directing battalion,

having assured his lieutenant-colonel on the perpendicular, will promptly establish two markers behind his battalion, as prescribed in the *S. B.*, No. 650.

433. The general will verify the direction of these markers, rectify it if necessary, and charge an officer to superintend, pending the march, the successive replacing of them.

434. The general will then command:

2. *Battalions forward.*

435. This command having been repeated, the color-rank of every battalion will advance six paces, and its two general guides will place themselves out abreast with this rank; the senior major will place himself at six or eight paces from the flank of the color-rank, and on the side opposite to the directing battalion.

436. The general need not occupy himself with the general alignment of the color-ranks and general guides of the different battalions; it will suffice if those of each battalion conform themselves to what has just been prescribed.

437. These dispositions having been made, the general will add:

3. MARCH (or *double quick*—MARCH).

438. At this, repeated with the greatest rapidity, the line will step off with life; each battalion will observe with the utmost care the principles prescribed in the *S. B.* for marching in line of battle.

439. Each colonel and lieutenant-colonel will conform himself, for the maintenance of the direction and alignment, to the principles prescribed in the *S. B.*

440. The directing battalion being regarded as infallible by all the others, and having thus the greatest influence on them, its march will be superintended with the utmost care; consequently, the general or the officer deputed by him, placed in front of this battalion, will labor to maintain its centre steadily on the perpendicular; to this end, he will frequently place himself from thirty to forty paces in front of the color-bearer, face to the rear, and align himself correctly on the markers established behind the battalion; he will rectify, if necessary, the direction of the centre corporal, as well as that of the color-bearer.

441. If the line of direction of this battalion be badly chosen, and this may often happen, as it is very difficult to determine the perpendicular with precision, the general and the colonel of this battalion will perceive it at the end of a few paces by the crowdings in one wing, and the openings of files in the other.

442. If, for example, the line of direction, instead of being perpendicular to the primitive line of battle, be taken to the right of the perpendicular, the directing battalion will soon be in an oblique position to both of those lines; the interval to its right will be more and more diminished, and that to the left increased in the same proportion, which will force all the subordinate battalions to oblique to the right to regain their intervals; the general, by placing himself on either flank of the directing battalion, will perceive that the battalions to its right are in advance, and those to its left in the rear, in respect to the false direction of that battalion.

443. Promptly to remedy this fault, the general will order the senior major of the directing battalion to place himself thirty or forty paces before its centre, and to face to the rear; he will himself go at the same time to a like distance behind its rear, and place, by signal of the sword, the senior major on the direction he may choose to give; the colonel of this battalion will immediately caution the centre corporal and the color-bearer to conform themselves to this new direction, and the officer superintending the markers in the rear will immediately establish them on that direction.

444. If, at the end of a few paces, the general perceive that the new direction is not exact, he will promptly give another; but with a good *coup d'œil*, and the habit of directing lines, he will rarely find it necessary to change the direction more than once.

445. Each subordinate battalion will maintain its interval on the side of the directing battalion.

446. The preservation of intervals between battalions being the most essential point in the march in line, the colonels will give to it the utmost attention.

447. A battalion can only lose its interval, from another, by the false direction pursued by its color-bearer. The colonel may early perceive this by the indications noticed Nos. 441-2, and as a remedy, he will apply the means indicated in the *S. B.*, No. 670 and following.

448. The interval may be momentarily diminished by openings between files; in this case, it will suffice to cause the files to close insensibly upon the centre of their battalion.

449. The general being further in rear of the line than the colonels, may see at once several battalions; hence it will be easy for him to perceive whence the loss of intervals, and he will give prompt notice thereof to the colonels.

450. When the loss of interval is but slight, and the battalion does not slant in respect to the perpendicular, the colonel may confine himself to cautioning the color-bearer to incline insensibly to the right or left, without taking the oblique step; by this means the interval may be re-established without inconvenience. As to the general alignment, the following rules will be observed.

451. A scrupulous attention need not be given to the maintenance of the colors and general guides of the several battalions exactly abreast with each other; consequently, the senior major of each battalion placed on the flank of his color-rank on the side opposite to the direction, will not cause the color-bearer to shorten or lengthen the step, but when this may be evidently necessary to the preservation of a certain degree of general harmony.

452. The two general guides of each battalion will conform themselves steadily to the direction of the color-rank of the same battalion, and hold themselves abreast with this rank, without deference to the colors and general guides of the other battalions.

453. Nothing contributes more to fatigue soldiers, and to derange the interior order of battalions, than frequent variations of step; the three corporals placed in the centre of each battalion will observe steadily the length and cadence of the pace, without endeavoring to maintain themselves exactly at the distance of six paces from the color-rank; consequently, they will not vary in either of those particulars except on a caution, to that effect, from their colonel or lieutenant-colonel.

454. To carry through the same principle, colonels will not scrupulously endeavor to maintain their battalions abreast with each other; consequently, they will not cause the step to be lengthened or shortened, the time to be marked or quickened, except when one or the other shall evidently be necessary in order to preserve a certain degree of harmony in the line; if it happen that a battalion find itself a pace or two in advance or in rear of the neighboring battalions, this slight irregularity may soon correct itself without particular orders or interference.

455. Colonels will carefully look to the direction and interior order of their respective battalions, and the lieutenant-colonels to the alignment.

456. The general will occupy himself more particularly with the directing battalion, but his attention will at the same time be given to the whole line.

GENERAL REMARKS ON THE MARCH IN LINE OF BATTLE.

457. The march in line of battle cannot be effected with the necessary order and harmony of parts, if the several battalions have not been previously and individually exercised according to the same principles or in the *S. B.*

458. Although uniformity of step be the first element in the march in line of battle, the movement will be imperfect if the color-bearer be not accustomed to prolong, without variation, a given direction, and if the colonels have not the habit of conducting their battalions with address and intelligence.

459. It is by the uniformity of step that the different battalions can alone maintain themselves, without effort, abreast, or nearly so, with each other, pending the march.

460. By exercising frequently, in advance, the sergeants as color-bearers, in prolonging a given direction, colonels may best prevent the loss of intervals in marching in line.

461. Finally, it is in forming the *coup d'œil*, by a persevering exercise, that generals and colonels can alone acquire accuracy and facility in judging the line of direction, and of conducting battalions on every sort of ground with the address and intelligence necessary to prevent faults, or promptly to correct them.

462. The general may choose, as the directing battalion, either in the line that he may judge the best posted for the particular march, yet, other considerations being equal, he ought to give the preference to a central battalion.

Article II.

To halt the line, and to align it.

463. The line being in march, and the general wishing to halt it, he will command:

1. *Battalions.*

464. This having been repeated, the general will add:

2. Halt.

465. This having been repeated with the utmost rapidity, the line will halt. The color-rank and general guides of each battalion, will halt, but remain in front of the line.

466. The line being halted, and the general wishing to give it a general alignment, he will place himself some paces on the right of the directing color, in order the better to see the whole line, and thence to determine the new direction.

467. He will next order the color-bearer and the left general guide of this battalion to face to him, when he will place them on the direction he shall have chosen; the right general guide will face to the left, and align himself on the color-bearer and the left general guide of the same battalion; the lieutenant-colonel will assure him on this direction, and the two corporals of the color-rank will fall back into their places in the line of battle.

468. The basis of alignment being thus assured, the general will command:

EVOLUTIONS OF A BRIGADE—PART V.   97

1. *Colors and general guides on the line.*

469. This having been repeated, the color-bearers and general guides of all the battalions will face to the color of the directing battalion: those of the next battalion to the right and left, respectively, will align themselves correctly on the color and general guides of that battalion; those of the other battalion will align themselves on the colors; the lieutenant-colonel and senior major of each battalion, will promptly assure the color-bearer and general guides of their battalions on the new direction: all the bearers will carry their colors perpendicularly between their eyes, and the corporals of their rank will fall back into their places in line.

470. These arrangements being made, the general will add:

2. *Guides on the line.*

471. This having been repeated, it will be executed in conformity with what is prescribed in the *S. B.*, No. 706 and following; and as soon as the guides are assured on the line, each colonel will cause his battalion to be aligned upon its centre without regulating itself on the other battalions.

472. All the battalions being aligned, the general will command:

3. *Colors and guides*—POSTS.

473. If the new direction should throw one or

more battalions back from the position occupied at halting, each colonel of these battalions, as soon as he perceives the necessity by the direction of the colors, will face his battalion about, march it to the rear, and then face it about when it has passed the new direction.

Article III.

Change of direction marching in line of battle.

474. A deployed line, marching in the order in battle, when the general shall wish to cause it to change direction, so as to throw forward a wing, the movement will be executed as follows.

475. If the left wing be the one intended to be thrown forward, the general will go to the right battalion, and place before it, on the new direction he may wish to give to the line of battle, two markers, distant from each other fifty or sixty paces, the first marker at the *point d'appui* for the right of the line; the markers being established, he will cause the line to be prolonged by mounted officers.

476. These dispositions made, the general will command:

1. *Change direction to the right.* 2. MARCH (or double quick—MARCH).

477. At the command *march*, briskly repeated, the movement will commence: each battalion will change direction according to the principles prescribed in the *S. B.*, No. 718 and following:

parallel
will then
thin the
general

ides will
t of the
the new
onel will
the cen-

y disen-
ill add:
will re-

lion will
illelly to
cause it
of direc-
ard the

idvance,
upon it

g halted
ew line,
des—ON

general
e to the
the line
rear of
correctly
ing exe-

Evolutions of a Brigade.

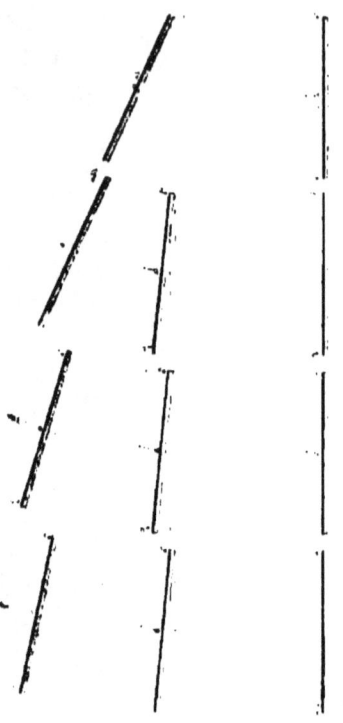
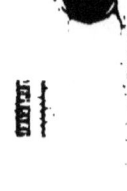

Change of direction marching in line of battle. No. 47.5

the right battalion will wheel until it is parallel to the new line of battle; its colonel will then direct it forward, halt it four paces within the markers, and command: 1. *Color and general guides*—ON THE LINE.

478. The color-bearer and general guides will face to the general placed on the right of the line, who will then establish them on the new direction; which being executed, the colonel will add: 2. *Guides*—ON THE LINE. 3. *On the centre*—DRESS.

479. As each battalion has sufficiently disengaged itself by wheeling, its colonel will add: *Forward*—MARCH; at this, the battalion will resume the direct march.

480. The colonel of the second battalion will so direct it as to cause it to arrive parallelly to the new line; and to this end, he will cause it to execute successively slight changes of direction in proportion as it advances toward the line.

481. Its lieutenant-colonel will, in advance, place himself on the line, and establish upon it two markers, as indicated No. 475.

482. The colonel of the second having halted his battalion at four paces from the new line, will command: 1. *Color and general guides*—ON THE LINE.

483. At this, the color-bearer and two general guides of the second battalion will face to the right, and promptly place themselves on the line of battle. The senior-major, from the rear of the left general guide, will align them correctly on those of the first battalion; which being executed, the colonel will add: 2. *Guides*—On the Line; 3. *On the centre*—Dress.

484. Each of the remaining battalions will conform itself to what is just prescribed for the second.

485. The lieutenant-colonel of each battalion will precede it on the line, by about one hundred paces, and conform himself to what is prescribed for the lieutenant-colonel of the second.

486. The general, or the officer whom he may substitute, placed on the right of the line, will take care that the colors of the first two battalions are correctly assured on the new direction: and when the last battalion is established on the line, he will command:

3. *Colors*—Posts.

487. Changes of direction to the left, in order to throw forward the right wing, will be executed according to the same principles and by inverse means.

REMARKS ON CHANGES OF DIRECTION MARCHING IN LINE OF BATTLE.

488. The means prescribed for changing the direction of a line marching in the order in battle, whether to throw forward, or to refuse one of its wings, give the facility of establishing a line on any direction that may be deemed best, without breaking the battalions into subdivisions.

489. The battalions marching in echelons, are

reciprocally protected: and if, before the end of the movement, it should become necessary to re-form the line, the battalions not yet on the new direction, say the third and fourth, inclusive, may form themselves into a full line, by an opposite change of direction to the one they were engaged in executing. This line would form an angle with the first already established on the new direction.

Article IV.

To retreat in line of battle.

490. The line being halted, when the general shall wish to cause it to march in retreat, he will command:

1. *Face to the rear.*

491. This having been repeated, each colonel will command: *Battalion about*—Face; when the line will face about, each battalion conforming itself to what is prescribed in the *S. B.*, No. 731.

492. The general will then add:

2. *The* (—) *the battalion of direction.*

493. At this, the colonels and lieutenant-colonels will conform themselves, within their respective battalions, to what is indicated in the *S. B.*, No. 733; and the colonel of the directing battalion will cause markers to be established as

9*

prescribed No. 734 of the same school. These dispositions being made, the general will add:

3. *Battalions, forward.*

494. This having been repeated, the color-rank, the general guides of each battalion, the captains, covering sergeants, and file closers, will conform themselves to what is prescribed in the *S. B.* The general will then command:

4. MARCH (or *double quick*—MARCH).

495. The line will march in retreat according to the principles prescribed for advancing in line of battle.

ARTICLE V.

To halt the line marching in retreat, and to align it.

496. A deployed line, marching in retreat, will be halted by the same commands as a line marching in advance; and when the general shall wish to re-face it, he will command:

1. *Face to the front.*

497. This having been repeated, each colonel will command: *Battalion, about*—FACE; when the line will face about, each battalion conforming itself to what is prescribed in the *S. B.*, No. 745.

Article VI.

Change of direction in marching in retreat.

498. A deployed line, marching in retreat, if the general wish to cause it to change direction in order to refuse the one or other wing, he will cause the movement to be executed as follows:

499. It will be supposed that it is the left wing, become the right, that the general wishes to refuse; he will pass to the right battalion, now the left, and establish two markers before it on the new direction which he may wish to give to the line, in the manner prescribed for changing direction in marching in advance; he will then command:

1. *Change direction to the left.*

500. This having been repeated, the general will add:

2. MARCH (or *double quick*—MARCH).

501. This briskly repeated, every battalion will commence its change of direction according to the principles prescribed in the *S. B.*, No. 751.

502. The first battalion will wheel until it find itself parallel to the markers; the colonel will then march it forward, cause it to cross the line of battle, and when the front rank, now in the rear, shall have passed four paces beyond this line, he will halt the battalion, face it about, and establish it on the line by the commands and means indicated Nos. 482–3.

503. The colonel of each of the other battalions will direct it toward the line of battle as indicated Nos. 479-80, so that it may be parallel to this line several paces before arriving upon it; the colonel will then cause the battalion to pass the line, and when four paces beyond it he will halt and face the battalion about; he will then establish it on the line by the means prescribed for changing direction advancing.

504. The lieutenant-colonels will conform themselves to what is prescribed Nos. 481 and 485, and the general to what is indicated No. 486.

505. Changes of direction to the right, in order to refuse the right wing, become the left, will be executed according to the same principles, and by inverse means.

506. A deployed line on a march will be marched in retreat without halting, by the commands and means prescribed No. 490 and following, observing what follows. The command, *right about*, will be substituted for *face to the rear*, and the second and third commands will be omitted.

Article VII.

March in line of battle of a line of battalions in columns.

507. The march in line of battle of a deployed line, presenting many difficulties, particularly if the ground be not favorable, it may frequently be advantageous to ploy each battalion into column, and to cause the line to march in this order, pre-

interval

o break
centre
or by

general
ibed in
to col-
d.
peated,
mands
licated

.

itself
in the

ccord-
:alions

:.

:talion
at the
g bat-
iether

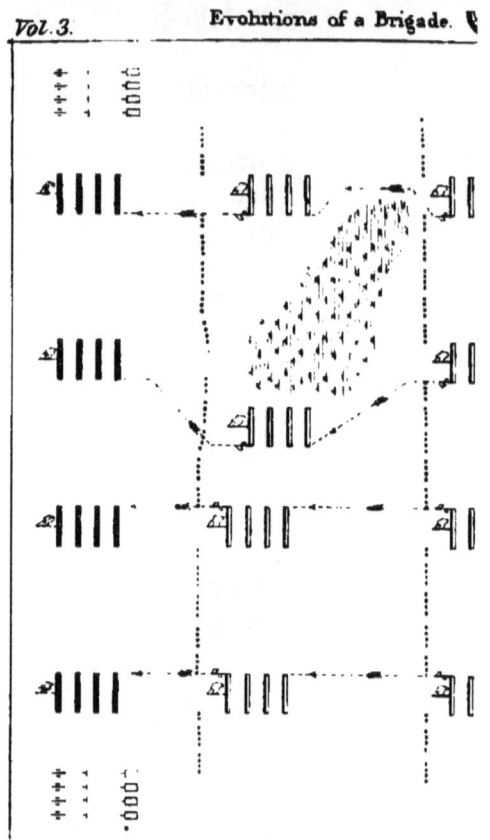

serving between every two battalions the interval necessary for deployment.

508. The general wishing to ploy or to break each battalion into column doubled on the centre or into simple column, either by division or by company, will command:

1. *Movement by battalion.*

509. This having been repeated, the general will give the commands of caution prescribed in the *S. B.* for the particular formation into column which he may desire to have executed.

510. These commands having been repeated, each colonel will give the preparatory commands required for the particular movement indicated by the general.

511. The general will then add:

2. MARCH (or *double quick*—MARCH).

512. At this, each battalion will ploy itself into column in the manner prescribed in the school of the battalion.

513. The line thus formed, will march according to the same principles as a line of battalions deployed, but observing what follows.

1st. *To cause the line of columns to advance.*

514. It will be supposed that each battalion has been ployed into double column, and that the general has chosen the third as the directing battalion: he will go to this battalion, see whether the direction of its guides be perpendicular to the line of battle, rectify the direction, if necessary, and then command:

1. *The third the battalion of direction.*

515. The colonel of each subordinate battalion having repeated this command, will see whether his guides on the side of the directing battalion be established perpendicularly to the line of battle; if not, he will make the necessary rectification, and then place himself thirty paces to the rear on the prolongation of those guides; the lieutenant-colonel will place himself a like distance in front, and on the same perpendicular.

516. The colonel of the directing battalion will establish in the rear two markers on the prolongation of the guides, as prescribed No. 432.

517. The general will now command:

2. *Battalions, forward.*

518. This having been repeated, the colonel of the directing battalion and the colonel to his left, will immediately command: *Guide right*, and the other colonels, *guide left.*

519. At this, the right general guide of each battalion will place himself six paces in front of its headmost guide; he will be assured on the perpendicular by the lieutenant-colonel, and immediately take points on the ground, as prescribed for the color-bearer, in the *S. B.*, No. 651; the lieutenant-colonel will then fall back to the side of his headmost guide.

EVOLUTIONS OF A BRIGADE—PART V. 107

520. The chief of each leading division will take post in the front rank of his division, on the flank opposite to that of direction, and the guide who was there will fall back into the rear rank.

521. The senior major will place himself in rear of the guides charged with the direction.

522. These dispositions being made, the general will add:

    3. MARCH (or *double quick*—MARCH).

523. At this, repeated with the utmost rapidity, the line will step off with life.

524. The right general guide of each battalion will direct his march perpendicularly to the front, and the leading guide will follow exactly in his trace.

525. The chief of the leading division will maintain himself abreast with his guide on the opposite flank, and see that the march of the division be in conformity with the principles prescribed in the *S. B.*, No. 667. The other divisions will conform themselves to the rules for marching in column.

526. The lieutenant-colonel and senior major will conform themselves to what is prescribed in the *S. B.*, Nos. 223–4.

527. Every colonel, placed on the side of direction, will superintend the march of his battalion in column, and labor to preserve its interval.

528. As the directing battalion has to be regarded as infallible by all the others, the general will attach himself to it, and with the greatest care maintain the general guide and guides of this battalion on the perpendicular, according to the principles established No. 440.

529. If the direction given to this battalion has been badly chosen, the general will promptly perceive it by the crowdings and openings among the files of the headmost division, according to the side to which the guide deviates from the perpendicular. Those irregularities, although less sensible than they would be in a deployed battalion, will nevertheless sufficiently show that the false direction of the general guide ought to be promptly corrected.

530. Colonels of the subordinate battalions will look with so much the greater care to the preservation of intervals, as a fault committed in this respect will not be as promptly perceived as in a deployed line.

531. In every battalion the lieutenant-colonel will perform the duty attributed to the senior major. in the *S. B.*, No. 671, as often as the colonel may wish to change the point of direction.

532. The line of battalions in columns being in march, when a subordinate battalion encounters an obstacle, this battalion will turn it in a manner so as to deviate the least from the direction it ought to follow, and take the double quick step as prescribed in the *S. B.*, No. 761, in order to return into line as soon as the obstacle is passed. When again in line, the battalion will be careful to re-establish its interval by insensible degrees.

533. If it be an interior battalion that has to execute the passage of an obstacle, the next battalion toward the side of the direction will take care to keep a double interval until the former battalion comes again into line.

REMARKS ON THE MARCH OF A LINE OF BATTALION COLUMNS WITH DEPLOYING INTERVALS.

534. It has been supposed above, that the battalions of the line were ployed into double columns; but the rules just prescribed are equally applicable to a line of battalion columns formed in any other manner.

535. When the battalions of the line are in simple columns, the directing battalion will take the guide to the left or right, according as it may have the right or left in front, and the subordinate battalions will take the guide on the side next to the directing battalion.

536. With the right in front, the right general guide in each battalion will be charged with its direction; the left general guide in the reverse case.

537. If the battalions be in masses, each colonel will hold himself, pending the march, at thirty paces in the rear of his battalion on the prolongation of its guides; the columns being at half distance, each colonel will hold himself on the flank of his column on the side of the direction.

2d. *To halt the line of columns, and to deploy it.*

538. A line of battalions in columns will be

halted by the same commands as a line of battalions deployed.

539. The line being at a halt, if it be the wish of the general to give a general alignment, he will conform himself to what is prescribed No. 363 and following.

540. If the battalions be in columns at half distance, and the general shall wish to deploy them, he will halt the line by these commands:

1. *Columns, close in mass.* 2. March (or *double quick*—March).

541. At the command *march*, each battalion will close up on its leading subdivision.

542. The line being halted and aligned, if it be the wish of the general to deploy the battalions, and they are in double columns, he will command:

1. *Deploy columns.* 2. March (or *double quick* —March).

543. If the battalions be in simple columns, the general will, in his first command, designate the subdivision on which each battalion ought to deploy itself.

544. In both cases, the movements will be executed, in every battalion, in the manner prescribed in the school of the battalion.

545. If the general does not wish to halt the battalion columns when they close in mass, and should he also wish to deploy while on the march,

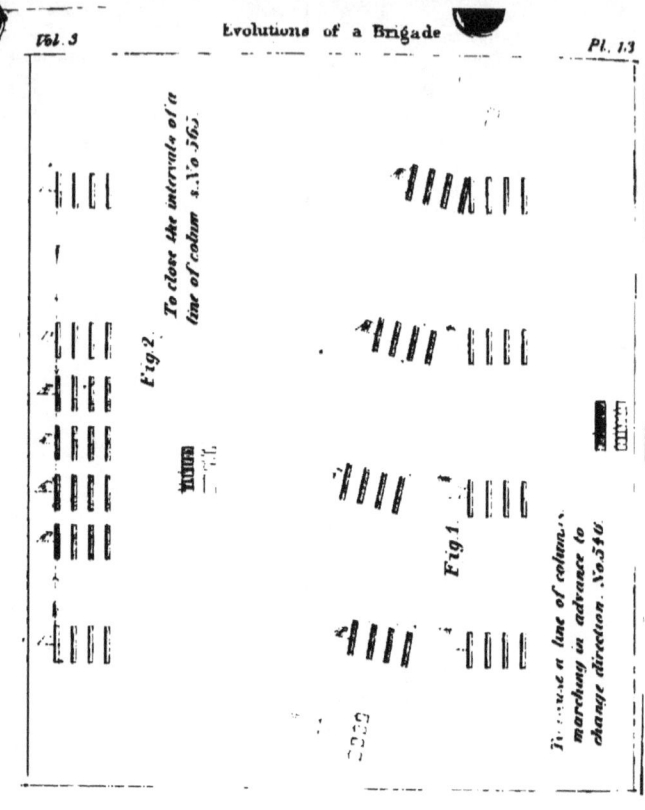

the movements will be executed according to the principles prescribed in the *S. B.*

3d. The line of columns marching in advance, to cause it to change direction.

546. A line of battalions in columns, marching to the front, and it being the wish of the general to cause it to change direction to the right, he will establish two markers on the new line of battle in front of the position to be occupied by the right battalion; he will at the same time charge two mounted officers to determine successively, in the manner indicated No. 264 and following, the points at which the other battalions ought respectively to arrive; these dispositions made, he will command:

1. *Change direction to the right.* 2. March (or *double quick*—March).

547. The first command having been repeated, each colonel will cause his battalion to take the guide to the right, if that be not already the directing flank; at the same time the chief of the leading division in each battalion will place himself before the centre of his division, and the general guide, charged with the direction, will retire. If the columns be closed in mass, the colonel of the first battalion will cause his battalion to take the guide to the left.

548. At the command *march*, the colonel of the right battalion will cause it to change direction to the right, and then direct it against the two markers placed by the general; when its leading division is at three paces from the markers, the colonel will halt the battalion; if the rear divisions have not yet entered the new direction, their chiefs will promptly bring them into it, and as soon as they are established on it the colonel will align the battalion by the right.

549. Each of the other colonels will direct his battalion toward the new line of battle, so that its leading division may be, when at a distance equal to the depth of a column, parallel to that line; to this end, the colonel will cause the guides of this division to advance, insensibly and successively, the left shoulder; and when this guide has arrived at three paces from the line of battle, the colonel will halt the battalion, and cause it to be aligned by the right.

550. At the beginning of the movement, the lieutenant-colonel of the second battalion will place himself on the line of battle, and replace the mounted officer whom the general had sent thither; he will immediately establish two markers for the head of his battalion, the first at deploying distance from the battalion to the right, and the second at division distance from the first: the lieutenant-colonel of each of the other battalions will place himself in like manner on the line of battle, when the head of his battalion is at a hundred paces from this line.

551. The last battalion column being established on the line. the general will command:

3. *Guides*—Posts.

552. Changes of direction to the left will be executed according to the same principles and by inverse means.

553. If the general shall wish to cause the columns to deploy, he will give the order to that effect to the colonels, who will cause their battalions to close up in halting, and then deploy them.

4th. To cause the line of columns to march in retreat.

554. A line of battalions, in columns, being halted, when the general shall wish to cause it to march in retreat, he will command:

1. *Face by the rear rank.*

555. This having been repeated, each battalion will face by the rear rank; the chief of the last division of each battalion will place himself in the rear rank, become the front on the side opposite to that of the direction; the chief of each first division will take his place in the column.

556. The line being thus faced by the rear rank, it will be put in march by the same commands and means as a line of battalions in columns faced by the front rank, observing to establish markers before the directing battalion, according to the principles prescribed in the *S. B.*, No. 734.

557. The line marching in retreat will conform itself to the principles prescribed for a line of battalions in columns marching in advance.

5th. To halt the line of columns marching in retreat, and to align it.

558. The line marching in retreat will be halted by the same commands as if it were marching in advance; and when the general shall wish to face it about, he will command:

1. *Face by the front rank.*

559. This having been repeated, each battalion will be faced by the front rank; the chief of the first division in each will retake his place in line, and the chief of each last division his in column.

6th. The line of columns marching in retreat, to cause it to change direction.

560. The line, marching in retreat, will change direction by the same commands and means as if it marched by the front rank, observing what follows.

561. The two markers established by the general before the position to be occupied at halting by the first battalion, instead of being opposite to the right and left files respectively of the leading division, will be far enough apart to permit this battalion to cross the line of battle between them, and the same of the markers established for the other battalions.

562. Each colonel will direct his battalion toward the line of battle as prescribed for a change of direction forward and so that all its divisions

EVOLUTIONS OF A BRIGADE—PART V. 115

may be parallel to this line before passing it; when the first division, now in the rear, is three paces beyond the line, the colonel will halt the battalion and face it by the front rank; the guides of the first division will place themselves on the line between the two markers; and as soon as they are assured in their positions by the lieutenant-colonel, the colonel will align the battalion by the right.

563. The general, if it be his wish to deploy the columns, will give a caution to that effect to the colonels, who, in halting, will each cause his battalion to close up on its leading division as soon as the latter has passed the line of battle by a distance equal to the depth of the column and three paces more; he will then face the battalion by the front rank and deploy it.

564. The line of battalion columns, in march, can be marched in retreat without halting, as prescribed No. 385. The colonel of each battalion will see that his interval is maintained.

7th. To close the intervals of a line of columns.

565. The line of columns, either simple or double, being at a halt, if the general should wish to close the intervals between them to twenty-two paces, on any battalion, say the third, he will cause two markers to be placed in front of that battalion, as indicated No. 411.

566. These dispositions being made, the general will command:

1. *On the third battalion close intervals.* 2. MARCH (or *double quick*—MARCH).

116   EVOLUTIONS OF A BRIGADE—PART V.

567. At the first command, the colonel of the third will caution his battalion to stand fast: the colonels of the first two battalions will command: 1. *Left face.* 2. *Battalion forward, guide right.* The colonel of the fourth will command: 1. *Right face.* 2. *Battalion forward, guide left.*

568. At the command *march*, briskly repeated, the colonel of the third will establish his battalion as prescribed No. 295, the others will march their battalions straight-forward, and having closed the interval which should separate them from the battalion on their left or right respectively, to twenty-two paces, will each halt his battalion, face it to the front, and dress it on the markers established by the lieutenant-colonels.

569. The lieutenant-colonels of the battalions, other than the third, will execute what is prescribed No. 416.

570. The movement being ended, the general will command:

3. *Guides*—Posts.

571. These battalions may again be made to resume their positions in line of battle, with deploying intervals, by the commands and means prescribed No. 411 and following.

572. A line of battalions in mass, can be closed or opened while on a march, by the commands and means prescribed No. 565 and following, and No. 411 and following, observing what follows. The line will not be marked in advance, and the colonels on the right and left of the directing battalion, will establish their battalions at the proper intervals, by causing them to oblique to the right or left, as the case may be.

Article VIII.

March in line of battle, of a line of deployed battalions, by the flanks of companies.

573. A line of deployed battalions, either at a halt or in march, will advance or retire by the flanks of companies, by the commands prescribed, and according to the means indicated No. 507 and following.

574. The line thus formed, either at a halt or on a march, advancing or retiring, will be re-formed by the commands prescribed in the *S. B.*, No. 150 and following, and means indicated No. 507 and following, of these evolutions.

Article IX.

March in line of battle, of a line of battalions formed in division columns.

575. A deployed line, either in a halt or on the march, will advance or retire, in division columns by the commands and means indicated No. 507 and following.

576. Double columns will be formed from the division columns, and reciprocally, as prescribed in the school of the battalion. The division columns will deploy, as prescribed in the same school.

REMARKS ON THE DISPOSITION OF THE ARTILLERY WITH LINES OF BATTLE.

577. If the march is in line, without the active sphere of battle, the brigade battery will follow the movement in its place; but if a position is to be attacked, the battery will cover the march of the troops, engage the enemy, and prepare for the attack.

Article X.

To pass a defile in front.*

578. A deployed line encountering, in advancing, a defile which it has to pass, will execute the movement as follows:

579. It will be supposed that the defile is opposite to the interval between the second and third battalions, and that its width is sufficient to give passage to the front of a company: the general, seeing that the line has arrived near the defile, will halt it, and command:

1. *To pass defile in front, by the right of the third battalion.* 2. *By platoon, left and right, into column.*

580. These commands having been repeated, the colonels of the first two battalions will each command: *By platoon, left wheel*, and the other colonels: *By platoon, right wheel.*

581. The general will then add:

3. March (or *double quick*—March).

Vol. 3. Pl. 24.

To pass a defile in front
Nº 579

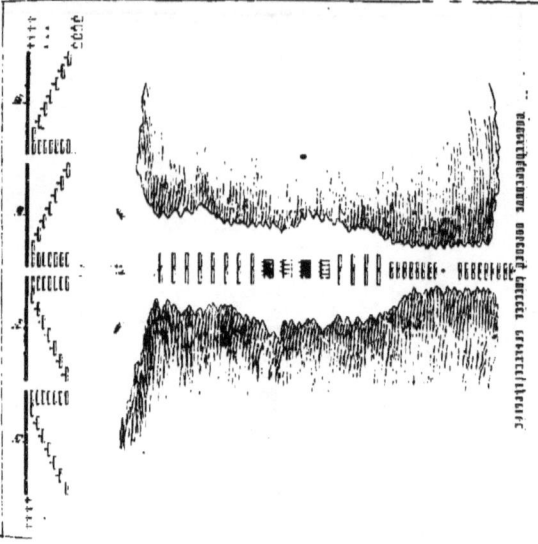

582. At this, briskly repeated, the battalions will break by platoon to the left or right.

583. The battalions having broken, the general will cause two markers to be placed at the points around which the two columns ought to turn in order to enter the defile; the markers will be posted a little more than the front of a company apart. The general will then command:

4. *Column, forward.*

584. This having been repeated, each colonel, whose battalion has broken to the left, will command: *Guide right,* and each whose battalion has broken to the right, *guide left.* The general will now add:

5. March (or *double quick*—March).

585. At this command, briskly repeated, the two columns will march to meet each other, and when the two leading platoons have arrived opposite to the respective markers, they will turn one to the right, and the other to the left, in order to unite in the defile; at the moment of union, they will take, by command of their respective chiefs, the platoon on the right, the guide to the left, and the left platoon, the guide to the right.

586. The two united platoons will march side by side, each regulating itself on the two guides placed elbow to elbow between them: these guides will direct themselves by the defile.

587. The two next platoons, and, successively, all the others, will conform themselves to what has just been prescribed for the two leading platoons on coming up with the markers placed before the entrance of the defile. If there is an odd battalion, it will form in simple column by company, behind the column nearest to it.

588. The united platoons will pass the defile in the cadenced pace, and with ranks closed, each regulating itself on the two guides placed in the centre, who will march elbow to elbow exactly in the traces of, and at platoon distance from, the guides who immediately precede them.

589. In proportion as the two columns issue from the defile, each captain will re-form his company as follows: in the right column, the first platoon, which is in rear of the second of the same company, will oblique to the right until it find itself unmasked, and then march forward: in the left column, it will be the second platoon of each company, which will oblique to the left, and then march up abreast with its first.

590. If it be the wish of the general, after passing the defile, to re-form the line, he will, immediately after passing, place himself in advance at the distance to which he may wish to establish the line of battle, and place two markers on this line for the head of the right column, and the two others for the head of the left, leaving the interval of twenty-two paces between the two columns.

591. The head of the column having passed the defile, the general will order the colonels of the second and third battalions to direct them respectively on the markers which he has established; and when the leading subdivision of each of these battalions has arrived at three paces from the line of battle, each colonel will cause his battalion to close in mass in halting, and deploy their battalions, the second on its last, and the third on its first subdivision.

592. The colonels of the first and fourth will each, as the head of his battalion issues from the defile, cause it to change direction, the first to the right, and the fourth to the left, and then direct it perpendicularly toward the line of battle, the first at twenty-two paces from the right of the second, and the fourth the same distance from the left of the third. In halting, at three paces from that line, each battalion will be closed in mass on its leading company, and will then be deployed, the first on its last, and the fourth on its first subdivision.

593. If, instead of re-establishing the line, as in the preceding example, it be the wish of the general to rest one of the wings, say the right, at the defile, he will cause both columns to take the guide to the right, and halt them the instant that the first company of the first battalion in the right column issues from the defile: this column, composed of the first and second battalions, will then be formed *to the right*, and the left column, composed of the third and fourth battalions, will close to half distance in marching, and form *on the right* into line of battle.

594. If it be the left wing that is to rest at the defile, the line may be formed according to the same principles, and by inverse means.

VOL. III.—11

REMARKS ON THE PASSAGE OF DEFILES IN ADVANCING.

595. The two columns being formed by platoon, if the defile should widen sufficiently, companies may be formed in each column without waiting till the head has issued from the defile.

596. When a sudden narrowing of the defile shall oblige the chiefs of platoon to break off, for the moment, one or two files to the rear, this diminution of front, as an exception to the rule established in the *S. C.*, No. 310, will be made from the side opposite to the guide.

597. If the defile be of sufficient width to receive the front of a division, the general, instead of causing the line to break by platoon, will cause it to break by company; but, in this case, the company that is to lead in each column, instead of wheeling, will march forward twice the extent of its front; and when the columns are put in movement, these companies will close upon each other, marching by the flank, in order to unite at the entrance of the defile.

598. If the defile be not of sufficient width to receive the front of a company, it will be passed in simple column by platoon, right or left in front.

599. The passage of defiles to the front will always be executed by the subdivision of the right, or that of the left of a battalion; and when the defile happens not to be exactly opposite to an interval between two battalions, the leading subdivisions, after uniting, will direct themselves diagonally toward the entrance of the defile.

EVOLUTIONS OF A BRIGADE—PART V.

REMARKS ON THE DISPOSITION OF THE COMPANIES OF SKIRMISHERS IN PASSING A DEFILE TO THE FRONT.

O-600. Generally, the skirmishers of each battalion will precede their battalion companies in passing a defile to the front. In this case, the companies of skirmishers of each battalion, under the command of the junior major, will pass the defile either by file, platoon or company front, as the width may admit, those of the battalions nearest the defile passing first.

O-601. If, however, the skirmishers are required to pass the defile with their battalions, the first company of each battalion will be posted in front or rear of its first battalion company, closed up on that company, and with a platoon or company front, as the column may be formed by platoon or company. The second company of skirmishers will be posted in like manner in front or rear of the last battalion company.

REMARKS ON THE PASSAGE OF THE DEFILE IN FRONT BY THE SECOND LINE.

602. If the formation is in two lines, while the first line is passing the defile the general will cause each battalion of the second line to form by company or platoon, according to the manner in which the first line may have broken. After the first line has passed the defile, the corresponding battalions of the second will pass in a similar manner.

Article XI.

To pass a defile in retreat.

603. The line marching in retreat, and encountering a defile which it has to pass, the general will cause a halt, and face the line to the front.

604. It will be supposed that the defile is opposite to the interval between the two centre battalions, and its width sufficient to give passage to the front of a company. The general will cause two markers to be placed at fifteen or twenty paces behind the file closers, in front of the defile, and at a little more than company distance apart, in order to indicate to the two columns the points around which they ought to change direction to enter the defile: which being executed, he will command:

To the rear, by the wings, pass the defile.

605. This having been repeated, the colonel of the right battalion of the line will command: *to the rear, by the right flank, pass the defile;* and the colonel of the left battalion, *to the rear, by the left flank, pass the defile.*

606. The two battalions of the wings will immediately commence the movement in conformity with what is prescribed in the *S. B.* No. 790 and following; and when the leading platoon of each column has arrived opposite to the marker placed at the point for changing direction, these two platoons will turn at the same time, one to the

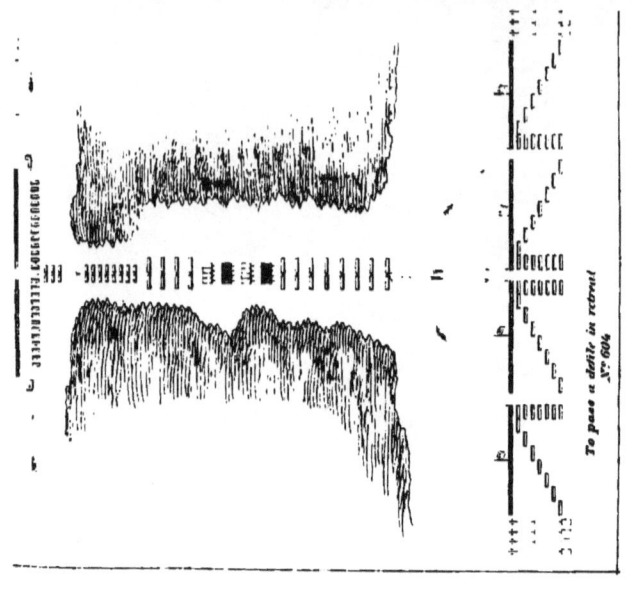

To pass a defile in retreat
Nº 604

left and the other to the right, in order to unite in the defile. To this end, if the head of one of the columns arrive before the other, it will wait for the head of the corresponding battalion before turning. As soon as the two platoons unite, they will take, by command of their respective chiefs— the platoon, now on the left, the guide to the right, and the other the guide to the left; the remaining platoons of these two battalions will successively conform themselves to what has just been prescribed for those of the head, and the two columns will thus march together according to the principles indicated No. 586* and following, for the passage of a defile in front.

607. The other battalions will successively execute the same movement; the colonel of each will give one of the commands prescribed No. 605, according as his battalion has to pass the defile by the right or left flank, and so that its leading platoon may follow at the desired distance, the rearmost platoon of the battalion immediately preceding; the battalions will enter the defile side by side, as prescribed for the two battalions of the wings.

608. If the defile become of sufficient width to give passage to a division marching by the front, each captain, as his platoons successively enter the enlarged width, will cause them to form company according to the principles prescribed No. 589; otherwise, this movement will only be executed as each company issues from the defile.

609. If it be the wish of the general, after passing, to re-form line facing to the defile, he will go either to the point at which he may wish the left of the first battalion to rest, or to the point at which he may wish the right of the fourth, or last battalion to rest, and determine the direction of the new line of battle by establishing two markers, distance from each other a little more than the front of a subdivision; he will then cause the line to be prolonged to the left and right by mounted officers.

610. As each battalion clears the defile, it will break from the column, and be directed toward the point at which it should cross the line of battle.

611. Each battalion will close in mass while marching, and be so directed as to arrive on a square with the line, and when four paces beyond it, will be halted by the colonel, countermarched, and deployed, the first and second battalions on their last, and the third and fourth battalions on their first subdivisions.

612. The lieutenant-colonel of each battalion will precede it, as prescribed in No. 269, and establish two markers, the first at deploying distance, and twenty-two paces from the one on his right or left, as the formation is on the left or right, the second a little more than subdivision distance from the first.

613. The defile, in the preceding example, has been supposed to be behind the centre of the line composed of an even number of battalions; but it may frequently be otherwise. For instance: it may be that there are three battalions on the right, and only one on the left side of the defile. In this case the general would first send an order to the colonels of the first and second battalions

to pass the defile in simple column in advance, and then seizing the proper time, give the command indicated No. 604, so that there may be no interruption in the movement. So, if the line present an odd number of battalions, a similar course would be pursued in respect to the odd battalion on the right or left of the defile.

614. When the defile happens to be behind the right or left battalion of the line, the general will cause it to pass by a single wing; to this end, he will substitute, in his command, the indication *by the left wing* or *by the right wing*, for that of *by the wings.* The movement will commence by the wing farthest from the defile, so that the battalion opposite to it may be the last to enter.

REMARKS ON THE DISPOSITION OF THE SKIRMISHERS IN PASSING THE DEFILE IN RETREAT.

0-615. If it is not the intention of the general to open the fire of the line before passing the defile in retreat, the skirmishers will generally cover the retreat, and not pass until the line has passed. If, on the contrary, the general intends to open the fire of the line, the skirmishers will generally pass the defile previous to the line, those of the battalions near the defile passing first.

REMARK ON THE PASSING OF THE DEFILE IN RETREAT BY THE SECOND LINE.

616. If the formation is in two lines, the general will, according to the width of the defile, and previous to passing the defile by the first line, cause each battalion of the second line to take the formation indicated No. 602. The battalions will then countermarch, and pass the defile previous to the first line, and as prescribed in the same paragraph.

REMARKS ON THE DISPOSITION OF THE ARTILLERY IN PASSING DEFILE IN FRONT, OR IN RETREAT.

617. In passing the defile to the front, the battery will habitually follow immediately after the first two battalion columns that pass.

618. In passing defile in retreat, should a stand be made by the line at its entrance, the battery, or a portion of it, will generally take a position to assist in sustaining the line, and will pass the defile immediately in front of the two last battalion columns. In case it is not intended that the line should make a stand, the battery will generally pass the defile in front of the battalion columns. The disposition of the battery must, however, depend greatly upon circumstances.

Article XII.

Changes of front.

Perpendicular changes of front.

1st. *Change of front forward.*

619. The line being deployed, and the general wishing to cause it to change front on the right,

V.

Evolutions of a Brigade

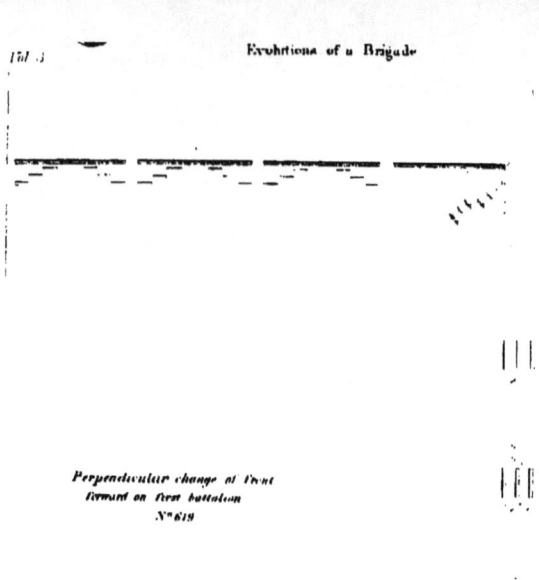

Perpendicular change of front
forward on front battalion
N.º 619

he will first determine the direction of the new line of battle, cause two markers to be placed on it before the position to be occupied by the right company, first battalion, and immediately cause this company to be established against those markers; he will at the same time charge two mounted officers to determine successively the points on the line at which the subordinate battalions ought respectively to arrive, as indicated No. 265 and following. He will then command:

1. *Change front forward, on the first battalion.*

620. This having been repeated, the colonel of the first will immediately cause his battalion to execute a change of front forward, as prescribed in the *S, B.*, No. 832 and following.

621. Each of the other colonels will cause his battalion to ploy into double column, at company distance; which being executed, he will command: 1. *Column forward;* 2. *Guide right.*

622. These dispositions being made, the general will add:

2. MARCH (or *double quick*—MARCH).

623. At this, briskly repeated, the subordinate battalions will put themselves in movement toward the line of battle; the leading guide of each, advancing the left shoulder, will so direct himself that, on arriving at a point opposite to the right marker, placed in advance by the lieutenant-colonel, he may find himself at a distance from the line of battle equal to the depth of the column.

624. The head of each battalion having arrived at this point will turn to the right, in order to march perpendicularly up to the line of battle, and when at three paces from this line, its colonel will cause the column to close in mass, and to deploy.

625. Each colonel will hold himself on the side of the direction, abreast with the leading division of his battalion, pending its march toward the line of battle.

626. The lieutenant-colonels will place themselves in advance on the line, as prescribed No. 550, for changes of direction of a line of battalions in columns.

627. The line being formed, the general will command:

3. *Colors*—Posts.

628. A line will change front forward on its left, according to the same principles and by inverse means.

2d. *Change of front to the rear.*

629. To change front to the rear, on the right of the line, the general will cause the right company, first battalion, to be established on the new direction, and place two markers before this company, as prescribed in the *S. B.*, No. 852, he will then command:

1. *Change front to the rear, on the first battalion.*

630. This having been repeated, the colonel of the first will immediately cause his battalion to execute a change of front to the rear, as prescribed in the *S. B.*, No. 854 and following.

631. Each of the other colonels will cause his battalion to ploy into double column at company distance, face it by the rear rank, and then command: 1. *Column, forward;* 2. *Guide left.*

632. These dispositions being made, the general will add:

2. MARCH (or *double quick*—MARCH).

633. This having been briskly repeated, the subordinate battalions will put themselves in movement toward the line of battle; the leading guide advancing the right shoulder, will direct himself as prescribed No. 623.

634. The leading division of each battalion having arrived at a point opposite to the markers, will turn to the left in order to march up perpendicularly to the line of battle, then cross this line between the two markers placed in advance by the lieutenant-colonel; and when the head of the battalion has passed the line a distance equal to its depth closed, and three paces more, the colonel will cause the column to close in mass, to face by the front rank, and to deploy.

635. The lieutenant-colonels will place themselves in advance on the line of battle, and establish upon it the two markers as prescribed No. 561.

636. Changes of front to the rear, on the left of the line, will be executed according to the same principles and by inverse means.

3d. *Central change of front.*

637. The general wishing to change front on the third battalion, by throwing forward the left wing, will cause two markers to be placed on the direction he may wish to give to the new line before the position to be occupied by the right company of that battalion, and then cause this company to be established against the markers; he will, at the same time, order the colonel of the second to have the left company of his battalion conducted to and established on the same alignment, at twenty-two paces from the right of the third battalion.

638. These dispositions being made, the general will command:

1. *Change front on the third battalion, left wing forward.* 2. MARCH (or *double quick—*MARCH).

639. The colonel of the third will immediately cause his battalion to execute a change of front forward on its right company, and the colonel of the second a change of front to the rear on the left company of his battalion.

640. The battalion to the left of the third will execute its movement as prescribed for the subordinate battalions in changes of front *forward* on the right of the line, and the battalion to the right of the second will execute its movement as indicated for changes of front *to the rear* on the left battalion. •

641. The general wishing to throw the right wing forward, instead of the left, will take, as the basis of alignment, the left company of the second battalion, and command:

1. *Change front on the second battalion, right wing forward.* 2. MARCH (or *double quick— MARCH.*

642. The second and the battalion to its right will execute a change of front forward, on the left of the second battalion.

643. The third and the battalion to its left, will execute a change of front to the rear, on the right of the third battalion.

Oblique changes of front.

644. Oblique changes of front will be executed according to the same principles as the perpendicular changes, but observing what follows:

645. The directing battalion will conform itself to what is prescribed in the *S. B.*, No. 872; the subordinate battalions, after being ployed into double columns, will be directed toward the new line of battle by the means indicated, No. 549 or No. 562, according as their change of front may be forward or to the rear.

646. If the line is in march, the changes of front will be executed by the commands and means prescribed No. 619 and following, and by the principles indicated No. 844 and following, and 872 and following, *S. B.* If the change is central, the battalions which should retire will halt at the commencement of the movement.

REMARK ON CHANGES OF FRONT.

647. In changes of front, the general will always take the right or left company of one of the battalions as the basis of the movement.

Changes of front of two lines.

648. If the formation is in two lines, the first will always execute its movements as if it were alone. The battalions of the second line, conducted by their colonels, will move to their proper posts, taking care to preserve their relative positions with the corresponding battalions of the first line.

ARTICLE XIII.

Order in echelon.

649. Echelons may be formed parallelly, or obliquely to the line of battle, either by the right or left of the line, and by battalion, or by two battalions, as will be explained.

Direct echelons in advancing.

650. The general wishing to form direct echelons by the right and by two battalions, will command:

1. *Echelons by two battalions, at* (so many) *paces.*
2. *Forward, by the right, form echelons.*

651. These commands having been repeated,

two right
the com-
d follow-
in battle,
alion.
st echelon
march of
e think it
placed be-
its direc-

succession,
intain be-
the num-
command;
of paces,
counted,

file closer,
elf in rear
preceding
exactly in
h his own
the right
ill always
n his own
preceding

helon will
pendicular
from the
will march
e care to

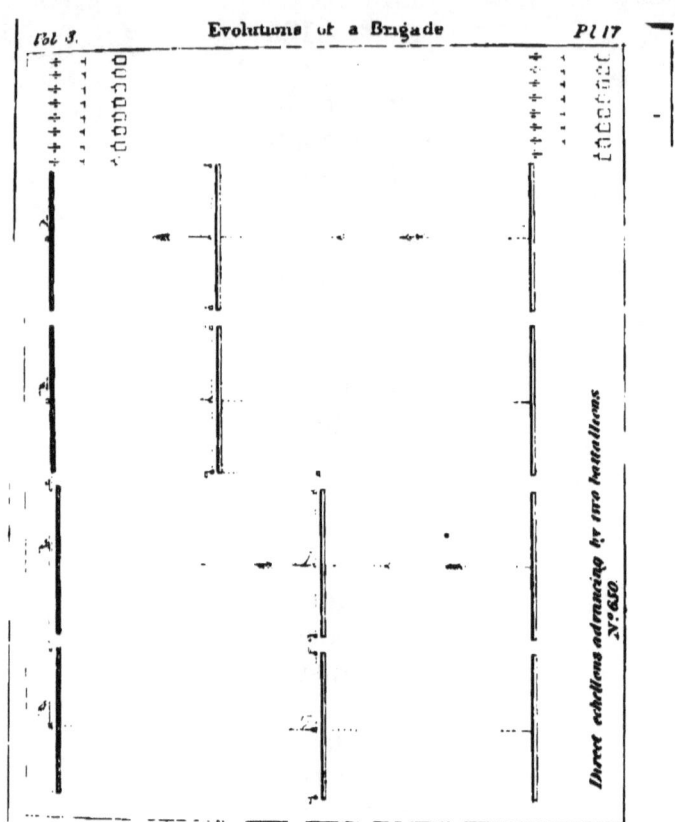

the ranking chief of battalion of the two right battalions will put them in march by the commands and means indicated No. 430 and following, for marching a line in the order in battle, and take the first as the directing battalion.

652. The right battalion of the first echelon becoming thus the regulator of the march of both the echelons, the general, if he think it necessary, will cause markers to be placed behind this battalion in order to assure its direction.

653. The second echelon will, in succession, put itself in march, observing to maintain between itself and the preceding echelon the number of paces prescribed in the first command; its commander will cause that number of paces, taken by the preceding echelon, to be counted, before putting his own in march.

654. In the subordinate echelon, a file closer, designated in advance, will place himself in rear of and opposite to the left file of the preceding echelon. This file closer will march exactly in the trace of that file and abreast with his own battalion; by this means, the chief of the right battalion in the subordinate echelon will always be able to maintain the interval between his own battalion and that on the left of the preceding echelon.

655. The right battalion in each echelon will be charged with preserving the perpendicular distance which ought to separate it from the preceding echelon; the left battalion will march abreast with that on its right, and take care to preserve its interval to the right.

656. The echelon being in march, when the general shall wish to re-form the line, he will give an order to the commander of the first echelon to halt it.

657. The first echelon being halted, the general will determine the direction to be given to the line, and the commander of the first echelon will establish it on that direction.

658. The second echelon will continue to march, and be successively halted by its chief at four paces from the line of battle.

659. The second echelon being halted, its chief will command: 1. *Colors and general guides—*On the line. At this, the colors and general guides of each battalion will face to the right, and promptly place themselves on the alignment of the colors of the first echelon; which being done, the commander of the second will add: 2. *Guides—*On the line. Each chief of battalion, seeing his guides established, will align his battalion.

660. Each chief of echelon will give the command, *Guides—*Posts, as soon as his echelon is aligned; but the colors will not fall back into their places until the general shall add: *Colors*—Posts, which will be given after the establishment of the last echelon on the line of battle.

661. If, instead of re-forming the line, it be the wish of the general to halt the echelons, he will give an order to that effect to the chief of the first, and send a caution to the chief of the second to halt his echelon in the position where it finds itself.

Vol 3   Evolutions of a Brigade

Direct echellons in retreat by two battalions.
N.º 663.

662. Echelons by the left will be formed according to the same principles and by inverse means.

Direct echelons in retreat.

663. It being the wish of the general to march in retreat by echelon of two battalions he will command:

1. *Echelons by two battalions, at* (so many) *paces.*
2. *In retreat, by the right, form echelons.*

664. These commands having been repeated, the commander of the first echelon will cause it to face about, and then put it in march.

665. The commander of the second echelon will cause it to face about, soon enough to be able to put it in march the moment it has its distance from the first.

666. The second echelon will throw out a file closer in the manner and for the purpose prescribed No. 654.

667. The general, wishing to re-form the line, will order the commander of the first echelon to halt it.

668. This echelon being halted, its chief will face it to the front, and establish it on the direction which may be indicated to him.

669. The second echelon will continue to march, and when at four paces beyond the line of battle, its chief will halt it, face it to the front, and establish it on the line by the means prescribed Nos. 659 and 660.

670. Echelons in retreat will be formed by

the left according to the same principles and by inverse means.

Oblique echelons.

671. It being intended to form echelons obliquely to the line of battle, the movement will be executed in the following manner.

672. Say that the movement is to be made by the right; the general will go to the right of the line, and determine the new direction according to his views.

673. The lieutenant-colonel of the right battalion will then on an intimation from the general, place himself before and near the right file of this battalion; then face to the left, march fifty paces along the front rank, halt, and face to his right; he will next march perpendicularly to the front of this battalion, counting his paces; the general placed on the right, will halt him the moment he comes between himself and the point of direction to the left of the new positoin, for the purpose of measuring the angle formed by the new and old directions.

674. It will be supposed that the opening of this angle is such, that the lieutenant-colonel, after marching fifty paces along the front of the battalion, had to take thirty perpendicularly forward, to bring himself in a line between the general and the point of direction to the left.

675. The opening of the angle being thus ascertained, the chief of the first echelon will immediately cause it to change front forward on its right company.

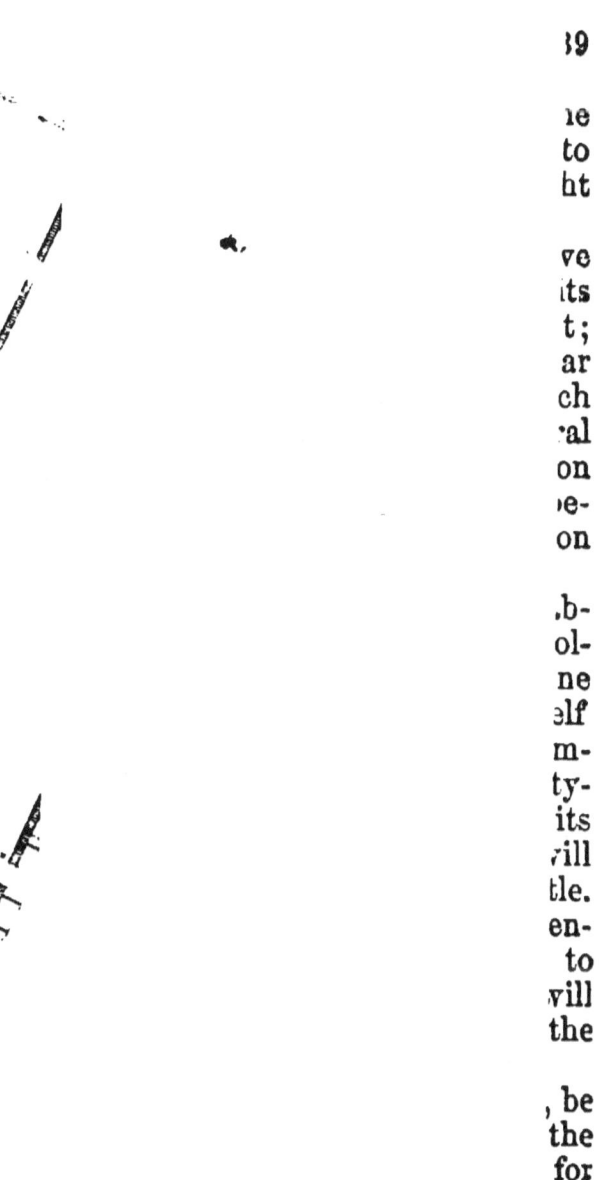

Evolutions of a Brigade.

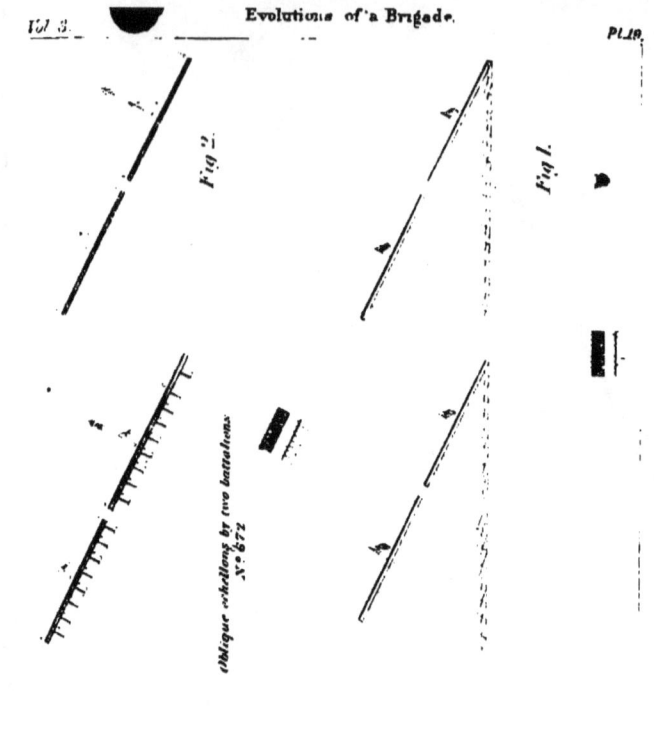

Fig. 2.

Fig. 1.

Oblique echelloning by two battalions
N.º 672

676. The general will then send an order to the other chief of echelon to cause his echelon to change front forward to thirty paces on its right company.

677. As the subordinate echelon shall have changed front, its chief will cause it to take its interval from the left of the echelon on its right; to this end, he will cause it to break to the rear into column by company by the left; which being executed, he will order the left general guide of the left battalion to place himself on the prolongation of the right guides a little beyond the point where the left of the echelon will rest when in line.

678. The general guide being correctly established, the chief of the echelon will put the column in march in order to prolong it on its line of battle; the leading guide will direct himself on the general guide, and when the right company, now in the rear, shall have passed twenty-two paces beyond the left of the echelon on its right, the chief of the echelon, in column, will halt it, and form it *to the right* into line of battle.

679. The echelons being thus formed, the general will order the chief of the first echelon to put it in march; the other chief of echelon will put his echelon in march as soon as he sees the preceding one in movement.

680. The echelons thus disposed will march, be halted, or re-formed into line, according to the principles prescribed No. 650, and following, for direct echelons.

681. Echelons will be formed obliquely by the left according to the same principles and by inverse means.

REMARKS ON THE ORDER IN ECHELON.

682. The distance between echelons cannot be fixed, the number of paces necessarily depending on the views of the general; but it ought to be such as to allow the battalion or battalions in the echelons to be formed into squares, without danger of their firing into the other echelons.

683. In the formation of oblique echelons, the distance between them will depend on the extent of their fronts and the angle formed by the old and new directions; this distance may be either too great or too small; if too great, the general, before putting the echelons in march, will give an order to the chief of the subordinate echelon to advance, and then halt it at the prescribed distance. If, on the contrary, the distance be too small, the subordinate echelon will only put itself in movement when it has the given distance from the one next in its front.

684. In changes of front, for the formation of oblique echelons, the angle formed by the old and new directions being necessarily acute, the subordinate battalion in each echelon will change front by the same means as the directing one, instead of ploying into double column in order to march and deploy on the new line.

685. The line of battalions, deployed, will habitually march in echelons; but if the general judge it to be more advantageous, he may ploy each battalion into column by division, in rear of its first division, if the echelons are formed by the right, and in rear of the last division of the battalion, if echelons be formed by the left.

686. When the echelons are composed of battalions in columns, if the movement be by the right, the file closer, who ought to march abreast with the directing battalion of the subordinate echelon, will place himself on the prolongation of the right guides of the left battalion in the echelon preceding his own, and march exactly in the trace of those guides. If the movement be made by the left, the file closer will place himself on the prolongation of the left guides of the right battalion in the preceding echelon.

687. If the formation is in two lines, each battalion of the second line will, in forming echelons, preserve its relative position with regard to its corresponding one of the first line. In this case, echelon by battalion would involve the movement of two battalions, and echelon by two battalions of the whole brigade.

Article XIV.

To retreat by alternate battalions.

688. The retreat by alternate battalions, or odd and even battalions, will be executed as follows:

689. The general, intending to execute the retreat by alternate battalions, will give information of his purpose to the two next officers in rank, who are respectively to command the lines of odd and even battalions, and at the same time indicate to the one who is to commence the movement the position in which he will halt his line. The general will then command:

1. *Retreat by alternate battalions.* 2. *Odd* (or *even*) *battalions, commence the movement.*

690. These commands having been repeated, the officer entitled to command the line of odd battalions, and which line it is supposed ought to commence the movement, will command:

1. *Odd battalions, face to the rear.*

691. This having also been repeated, the chiefs of the designated battalions will cause them to face about.

692. The commander of the odd battalions will then add:

2. *The* (—) *the battalion of direction.* 3. *Battalions, forward.* 4. MARCH (or *double quick*—MARCH).

693. At the command *march*, briskly repeated by the chiefs of the odd battalions, these battalions will commence the march, and direct themselves perpendicularly to the rear. The chief of the subordinate battalion will maintain it abreast with the directing one in conformity with what is prescribed No. 454, and when the line arrives at the position indicated by the general, the chief of this line will command:

1. *Battalions.* 2. HALT.

694. At the second command the line will halt, each chief of battalion will immediately face his

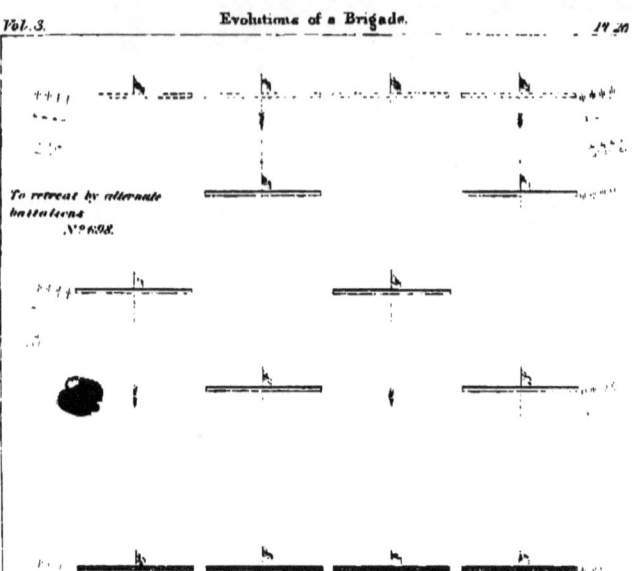

To retreat by alternate battalions.
N.º 698.

EVOLUTIONS OF A BRIGADE—PART V. 143

battalion about, the commander of the line will rectify the alignment of the directing battalion, the other battalion will be dressed by that, without constraint, however, as to being absolutely on the same general alignment.

695. As soon as the odd battalions which form the second line have faced about, the chief of the first line, of even battalions, will command:

1. *Face to the rear.*

696. This will be executed as prescribed No. 691; the chief of this line will then command:

2. *The (—) the battalion of direction.* 3. *Battalions forward.* 4. MARCH (or *double quick—* MARCH).

697. The first line will march in retreat by the means prescribed No. 693; each battalion will be directed upon the middle of the corresponding interval in the second line, cross this line, and march perpendicularly to the rear. When it arrives at the position indicated by the general, the first line will be halted and faced about by the commands and means indicated Nos. 693–4.

698. The second line, become first, will execute the same movement, and so on alternately.

699. The general will superintend both lines, and determine, according to the ground, the distance he may wish to have between the lines, and the position each ought successively to occupy.

To re-form the line.

700. The general, wishing to re-form the line, will cause the drums to beat a short roll, or the bugles to sound *the assembly*, after the first line (the one actually in front) is put in march, which roll or sound will be briskly repeated by all the drums or bugles of this line.

701. The battalions of the first line will continue to march, and when they find themselves exactly in their intervals of the second, their respective colonels will halt them, face them about, and rectify their alignment; the general will then give a general alignment if he judge it necessary.

REMARKS ON THE RETREAT BY ALTERNATE BATTALIONS.

702. The commander of each line will endeavor to maintain the necessary harmony between its battalions, notwithstanding the interval between them; to this end, he will look to the strict execution of what is prescribed Nos. 693 and 694.

703. He will more particularly see that the battalions, after crossing the second line, direct themselves perpendicularly to the rear, this being the only means by which the interval can be preserved with sufficient accuracy to enable the two lines to re-form into one.

704. If the formation is in two lines, the odd or even battalions of the second line will face about at the same time with their corresponding

rch to the
ing care to
ns and dis-

ARTILLERY
TALIONS.

y must de-
ction, but
line near-
on as will

te the pas-
the com-
the posi-

will form
disposed
pposite to
or left of
t line, ac-
ral.
posed, the
nander of
, and give
first line.
ill imme-

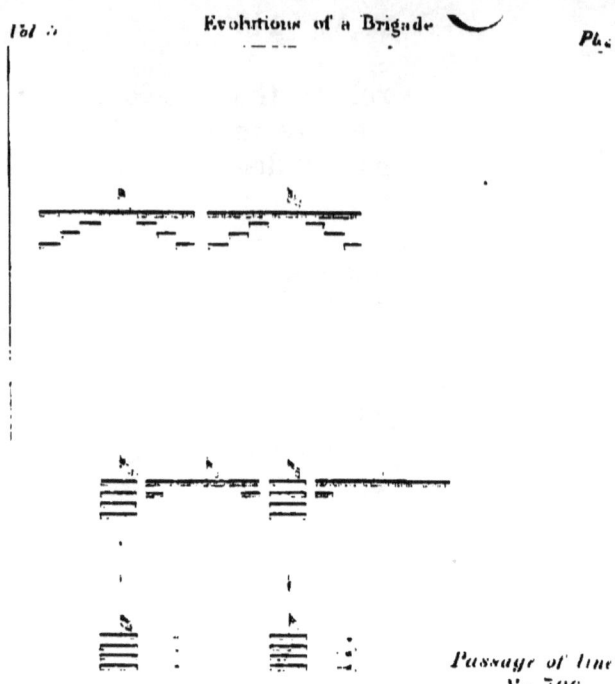

Passage of line
No. 706.

ones of the first line; they will march to the rear at the same time with them, taking care to preserve their proper relative positions and distances.

REMARKS ON THE MOVEMENTS OF THE ARTILLERY IN RETREATING BY ALTERNATE BATTALIONS.

705. The movement of the battery must depend much upon the state of the action, but generally it will keep abreast with the line nearest the enemy, and take such position as will most effectively cover the retreat.

Article XV.

Passage of lines.

706. The general, wishing to execute the passage of lines, will send an order to the commander of the second line to place it in the position it ought to occupy.

707. The battalions of this line will form double columns, closed in mass, and so disposed that the centre of each mass may be opposite to the middle of the interval to the right or left of the corresponding battalion of the first line, according to the order given by the general.

708. The second line being thus disposed, the general will send an order to the commander of this line, to execute the passage of lines, and give notice thereof to the commander of the first line.

709. The chief of the second line will immediately command:

1. *Pass the line in front.* 2. *Battalions, forward.*

710. These commands having been repeated, each chief of battalion will command: *guide centre.*

711. The commander of the line will then add:

3. MARCH (or *double quick*—MARCH).

712. At this, briskly repeated, the second line will advance; each battalion will direct itself upon the middle of the corresponding interval in the first line.

713. At the approach of the second line, each chief of battalion in the first will cause the right and left companies of his battalion to be ployed, as in mass, behind the contiguous companies, in time not to arrest the movement of the battalions of the second line.

714. The battalions of the second line will thus pass the first; and when they shall have cleared it, the commander of the second will designate the directing battalion. This battalion will take the guide to the right, and the subordinate battalion will take the guide on the side next to the directing battalion.

715. The battalions having arrived at the given position, the commander of the line will cause them to halt and to deploy, or they may deploy on the march, so as to finish their deployment at the required place of halting.

716. As soon as the second line has passed the first, the chiefs of battalion of the latter will cause the right and left companies of their respective battalions to return into line. They will then ploy their respective battalions, either in simple or double column, as the general may direct, and take their proper positions in rear of the corresponding battalions of the second line.

REMARKS ON THE DISPOSITION OF THE ARTILLERY IN THE PASSAGE OF LINES.

717. If the second line passes the first for the purpose of relieving the latter, the battery will take a favorable position to cover the movement and fire with the greatest rapidity, without changing its position while the movement is being executed.

718. If the first line is passed for the purpose of an offensive movement, the battery will take a position in advance of the line, and cover the movements of the troops.

Article XVI.

Dispositions against cavalry.

719. No matter what the number of battalions which compose a column or line, not more than one will be formed into the same square. The squares will generally be formed by echelons.

720. A brigade containing four battalions will be supposed in column, by company, at half distance. The general, wishing to form square, will first cause divisions to be formed.

721. If it is supposed that the general wishes to form echelons on one of the centre battalions, he will command:

1. *To form square.* 2. *Echelons by battalion at* (so many) *paces.* 3. *On* (such) *battalion right* (or *left*) *in front, form echelons.*

722. At this, the colonel of each battalion in front of the designated one will either command: *Battalion right face*, or, 1. *Guide left;* 2. *Head of column to the right;* and the colonel of each battalion in rear of the designated one will either command: *Battalion left face*, or, 1. *Guide right;* 2. *Head of column to the left*, as the general may have previously caused to be indicated.

723. These dispositions having been made, the general will command:

4. MARCH (or *double quick*—MARCH).

724. At the command *march*, the portion of the column which is to form the directing echelon will stand fast.

725. All the other echelons will put themselves in march at the same time, each taking its direction from the side of the directing echelon; and whether it march to the right or left, it will be halted by its commander when it has taken the given number of paces from the next echelon on the side of the direction.

726. At the commencement of the movement, the directing echelon will form square; the com-

Evolutions of a Brigade.   Pl. 22

To form square, echellon from column at (so many) paces.   N.º 721

Column against cavalry.
No. 731.

mander of each of the other echelons, after halting it, will rectify the alignment so that it may be parallel to the directing echelon, and then cause it to form square.

727. If the column is at full, instead of half distance, the general will first form divisions, and then close the column to half distance on any designated division, by the means heretofore indicated. He will then form square by echelon, as prescribed above.

728. If the column be closed in mass, the general will cause it to take company distance, on any division he may designate, by the means heretofore indicated. He will then form square by echelon, as prescribed above.

729. If the column at half distance is so immediately menaced by cavalry, that there is no time to place it in echelon, the general will command:

Form squares.

730. This having been repeated, each colonel will form his battalion into square on its ground.

731. When a column closed in mass, is so suddenly threatened by cavalry as not to allow time to take distances, it will be formed as follows. The general will command:

Column against cavalry.

732. This having been repeated, each colonel will form his battalion into square as prescribed in the *S. B.*, No. 1202 and following.

733. Squares will be marched, columns will be formed, and squares reduced, by the commands and means prescribed in the *S. B.*, No. 1049 and following; No. 1060 and following; No. 1086 and following, and No. 1207 and following.

To form square from line of battle.

734. The square from line of battle, will always be formed by battalion, and disposed in echelon if there is sufficient time. The perpendicular distance between the echelons will be such that, the squares being formed, the first front of the second may find itself at least fifty paces farther to the rear than the fourth front of the first echelon. This rule is equally applicable to a column to be formed into squares.

735. When the echelons have to march in advance or in retreat, they will be formed according to the principles prescribed No. 650 and following, whether the battalions, which are to compose the echelons, be already disposed for the formation of squares, or be yet deployed. If the echelons are to remain at a halt, they will be formed on the centre, or on one of the wings, as will be explained.

736. It is supposed that the general wishes to form the echelons on the centre, he will command:

1. *To form square.* 2. *Echelons by battalion at* (so many) *paces.* 3. *On* (such) *battalion right*

-PART V.

echelons.
ɪ).

;he portion
cting eche.
then exec
25.
ɩ the echel
louble colur
ds and me
ind followii
iis caution
ɩelon will l

lines, the l
·ɔ at the sa
s of the f
ɔ time. E
however,
er to the ri
onding one

lry, and wi
d in echel
ɜ by battal

ʔ. *On the fi*

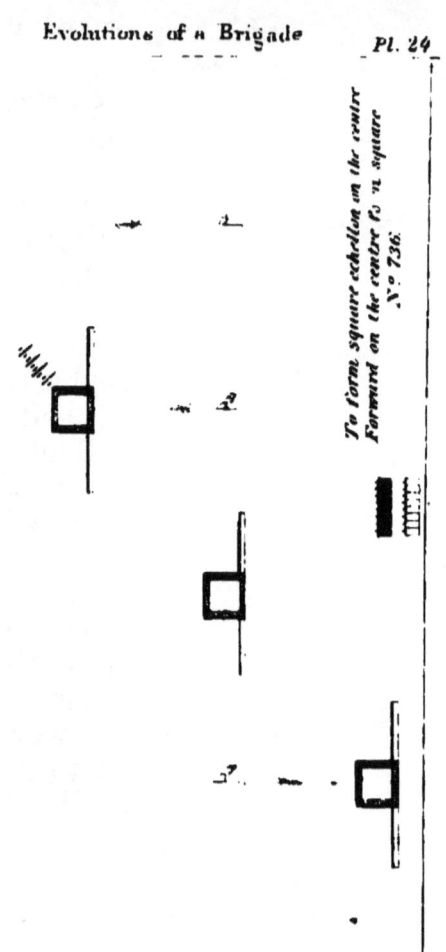

(or *left*) *wing in front from echelons.* 4. MARCH (or *double quick*—MARCH).

737. At the command *march*, the portion of the line which is to form the directing echelon, will stand fast. The echelons will then execute what is prescribed Nos. 724 and 725.

738. If the general should wish the echelons to form square, as if formed from double column, it will be executed by the commands and means prescribed in the *S. B.*, No. 1103 and following; each colonel taking care to give his cautionary commands in time, so that his echelon will halt in its proper place.

739. If the formation is in two lines, the battalions of the second line will move at the same time with the corresponding ones of the first line, and form square at the same time. Each battalion of the second line, will, however, before forming square, be moved either to the right or left, so as to unmask its corresponding one of the first line.

Oblique squares.

740. A line threatened by cavalry, and without time to form squares disposed in echelon, will be formed into oblique squares by battalion in the following manner:

The general will command:

1. *Oblique square by battalion.* 2. *On the first division, form square.*

741. At the second command, the colonel of each battalion will immediately form his battalion into oblique square on its first division, by the commands and means prescribed in the *S. B.*, No. 1167 and following.

742. The formation of battalions into oblique squares, on the left division of each, will be executed according to the same principles, and by inverse means.

743. In the preceding example the line was supposed to be deployed; but if it be formed of battalions already in columns with deploying intervals, the desired obliquity will be established by causing each battalion to change direction by the flank; to this end, the general will command:

1. *To form oblique squares by battalion.* 2. *Change direction by the right* (or *left*) *flank.*

744. At the second command, the lieutenant-colonel of each battalion will trace the new direction as prescribed in the *S. B.*, No. 1175. Pending this operation, each colonel will give the commands, and make the preparatory dispositions for a change of direction by the flank, and cause it to be executed as soon as the new direction is traced. The change of direction having been executed, he will cause the square to be formed.

745. A column at full distance may be formed into oblique squares by the same means: each battalion will be closed to half distance on its headmost subdivision; which being executed,

just

res,
he
he

nel
ex-
ace
the
ect-
wo
to
ght

en-

2.
CH

nel
he
ib-

ed,

Evolutions of a Brigade

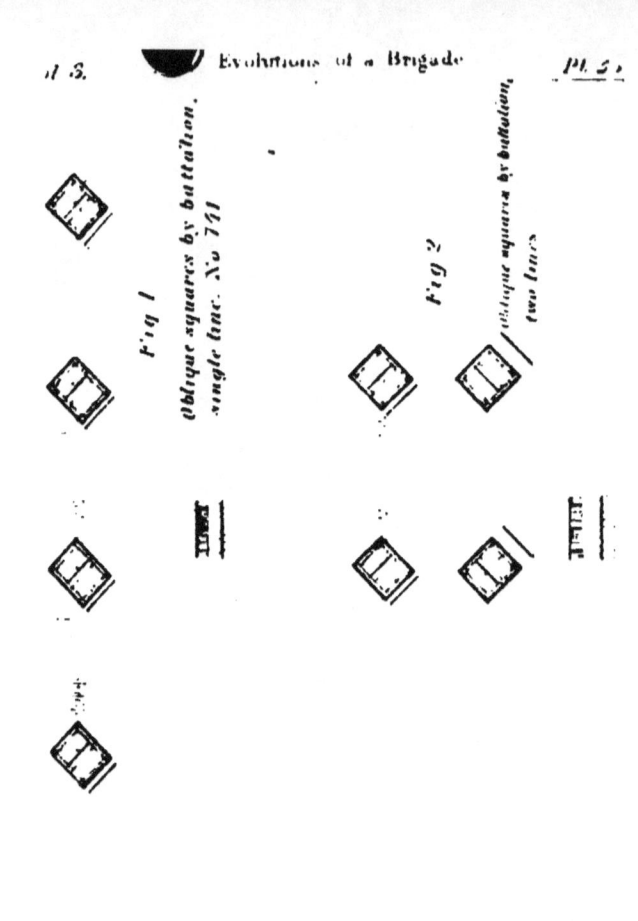

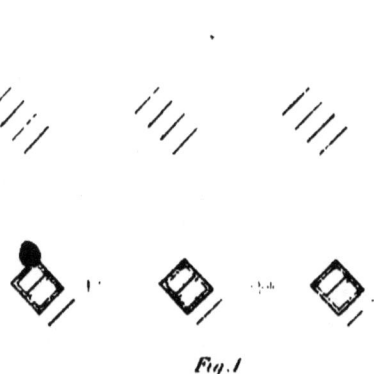

Fig.2

To re form the line
No 746

Fig.1

Oblique squares from line of columns
No 743

EVOLUTIONS OF A BRIGADE—PART V. 153

the battalion will change direction, as has just been prescribed, and then form square.

To re-form the line.

746. The line being disposed in oblique squares, when the general shall wish to re-form it, he will cause the squares to break; to this end, he will command:

1. *Reduce squares.*

747. At this, briskly repeated, each colonel will cause his square to break. Pending the execution of the movement, the general will place himself in front of the square he may judge the most conveniently situated to become the directing battalion, say the third; he will place two markers in the direction he may wish to give to the line, and cause it to be prolonged to the right and left, by the means prescribed No. 291.

748. These dispositions being made, the general will command:

1. *Form line of battle at* (such) *intervals.* 2. *The third the battalion of direction.* 3. MARCH (or *double quick*—MARCH).

749. At the second command, each colonel will give the commands indicated No. 421. The lieutenant-colonels will execute what is prescribed No. 423.

750. At the command *march*, briskly repeated,

the movement will be executed as prescribed No. 422.

751. The movement being ended the general will command:

4. *Guides*—Posts.

752. If the formation is in two lines, the battalions of the second line will form oblique squares on the positions they occupy, at the same time as those of the first line.

REMARK ON OBLIQUE SQUARES.

753. The formation of a line into oblique squares, gives the facility of placing it, whatever be its extent, as promptly in safety against the attacks of the cavalry, as if it were a single battalion, without causing the line to quit the position it occupies, and then, after re-forming each square into column, the line may be marched in any direction. The fires of oblique squares also cross each other in every direction, except that of the squares themselves, and this even when the battalions, before being formed into squares, happened not to be on the same alignment.

REMARKS ON THE DISPOSITION OF THE ARTILLERY WITH THE SQUARES.

754. If a cavalry charge is threatened, the battery will take up such positions as most effectively to fire upon the enemy, and at the same time avoid the fire of the squares. It may be found expedient, to concentrate all the pieces near the interior of the angle of the square nearest the enemy; or, the battery may be divided, and placed near the interior angles of the two squares of the first line, or between the lines.

755. As soon as the pieces are in battery the ammunition pouches will be filled, and the limbers and caissons sent to the rear of the second line.

756. If the gunners are driven from their pieces, they will take refuge in the nearest square. As soon as the charge is repulsed, they will immediately return to their pieces, and open fire upon the enemy.

END OF EVOLUTIONS OF A BRIGADE.

TITLE VII.

EVOLUTIONS OF A CORPS D'ARMEE.

General principles for the evolutions of a corps d'armee.

1. The evolutions of a brigade comprehending all the principles and details of the movements which should be made by a single brigade, it only remains to apply these principles to a *corps d'armée*.

2. In this instruction, a *division of the line* will be supposed to consist of three brigades, and in every line of battle composed of more than one of these divisions, they will be posted from right to left in the order of their numbers.

3. For the illustration of this instruction, a *corps d'armée*, consisting of nine brigades, will be supposed, but the rules herein prescribed are equally applicable to a *division of the line*, or to two or more brigades.

Posts of the general-in-chief, of the major-generals and brigadier-generals, in line and in column.

4. In line of battle *the general* (that is the particular general-in-chief) will have no fixed position; he will go wherever he may judge his presence necessary.

5. In column, he will hold himself habitually

corps d'armée
n réserve

at its head, in order to direct it according to his views.

6. In the evolutions, he will place himself at the point whence he can best direct the general execution of the movement.

7. In all cases the general may repair wherever he may judge his presence necessary, taking care to leave in his habitual position the next in command, or the chief of his staff, charged with the execution of his orders.

8. In line of battle, major-generals (generals of division) will place themselves at about one hundred and ten paces in rear of the centres of their divisions.

9. In column they will hold themselves on the directing flank, abreast with the centres of their divisions, and at sixty paces from the guides.

10. Brigadier-generals (generals of brigade) will place themselves as prescribed in the *E. B.*, Nos. 3 and 4.

11. Major-generals, will look to the exact and regular execution and transmission of all signals or notifications from the general, and commands or instructions given by themselves pursuant thereto; accordingly, they may repair wherever they may judge their presence necessary, within the extent of their divisions.

12. Brigadier-generals will look to the exact and regular execution of all signals, notifications, or commands coming from their major-generals, and to all commands given by themselves pursuant thereto; accordingly, they may repair wherever they may deem their presence necessary, within the extent of their brigades.

General rules for commands.

13. In *corps d'armée*, the evolutions and movements will be executed by means of signals, bugle sounds, and commands.

14. When the general shall wish a movement to be executed, he will send staff officers to notify the generals of division of the nature of the movement, or, he may make use of telegraphic signals to the same end. Each major-general will, then, by staff officers, immediately notify the brigadier-generals of his command of the movement to be made.

15. The general will then cause the *attention* to be sounded, which will be briskly repeated by the buglers of the major-generals, and, at which the generals of brigade will each immediately give by word of mouth the general commands relating to the manœuvre, and applicable to his brigade.

16. The final command, or that which determines the *execution* of the general movement, will always be given by the general, who to that end will cause the signal of *execution* to be sounded, which signal will be briskly repeated by the bugles of the major-generals.

17. The command of execution, signified by the sound, will be immediately given by the generals of brigade, and briskly repeated by the colonels, and, if necessary, by the lieutenant-colonels and majors, as prescribed in the *E. B.*, No. 12.

18. In case the generals of division or brigade have not been notified of a movement previous to the signal of *attention*, the signal of *execution* which follows, will indicate that the command is to advance to the front, in the then order of formation. The generals of brigade will give the preparatory command for forward, immediately after the signal of *attention*, and at the signal of *execution*, they will command *march*.

19. If during the march the general should wish to halt his command without having previously notified the generals of division, he will cause the signal of *execution* only, to be sounded, at which the generals of brigade will immediately halt their brigades. *This rule is general.*

20. When a line has to execute a central movement, the general will repair to the position which he may have selected as the *point d'appui*, and inform the generals of division of the manœuvre, as prescribed No. 14.

21. In column, commands will be extended by repetition, according to the same principles.

22. As often as a line breaks into several columns, the senior general officer, or colonel, in each, will discharge the duties attributed above to the general, or general-in-chief; but commands will not be given by signals or bugle sound, unless the column consists of more than one brigade.

PART FIRST.

Article I.

To open and to close ranks.

Article II.

Loading at will and the firings.

Article III.

To cause the line to rest.

23. The general wishing the movements prescribed by the above articles to be executed, will cause the generals of division to be informed of his intention, who will, in turn, notify their generals of brigade. The general will then cause the signal of *attention* to be sounded, at which each general of brigade will give the preparatory commands appropriate for the movement, as prescribed in the *E. B.*

24. The general will then cause the signal of *execution* to be sounded, when the generals of brigade will give the command which the signal indicates, and cause it to be executed as prescribed in the *E. B.*

PART SECOND.

DIFFERENT MODES OF PASSING FROM THE ORDER IN BATTLE TO THE ORDER IN COLUMN.

Article I.

To break to the front, to the right or left into column.

25. The movements prescribed by the above-named article, will be executed according to the principles indicated Nos. 23 and 24.

26. In breaking to the right (or left), to march to the left (or right), each general of brigade after the leading one, will take care to move his brigade, so that there shall be between the leading subdivision of his headmost battalion, and the rearmost subdivision in the preceding brigade, the distance of a subdivision and one hundred and fifty paces, in case the battery of his brigade moves in its rear.

27. When the column is at full distance, and the brigade batteries move within the columns of their respective brigades, in rear of the leading or three leading battalions, the distance between the leading subdivision of one brigade, and the rearmost subdivision of the one preceding, will be the length of a subdivision, and fifty paces if the column be formed by company, and a subdivision and ninety paces if the column be by division.

28. These distances in column between the

brigades, will result from the leading or three leading battalions, having moved forward to admit the battery, as prescribed in the *E. B.*, No. 216.

Article II.

To break to the rear by the right or left into column.

29. The line will be broken to the rear, according to the principles indicated Nos. 23 and 24.

Article III.

To ploy the line into column or in mass.

30. The general wishing to ploy the line, will cause the movement to be executed by the commands and means prescribed Nos. 23 and 24. Each general of brigade, at the signal of *attention*, will give the necessary preparatory commands for ploying in a proper manner his brigade as if by itself.

31. At the signal of *execution*, the ployments in each brigade will commence, and be executed simultaneously, and as soon as each brigadier has finished the ployment of his brigade, he will conduct it by the shortest route to its proper position in the general column.

32. To this end, those brigade columns whose places in the general column are in rear of the brigade of formation, may respectively be faced by the rear rank before commencing the march for positions in that column.

Vol. 3　　　　　　　　　　　　　　　Pl. 28.

Ploymouth
in two U
right of

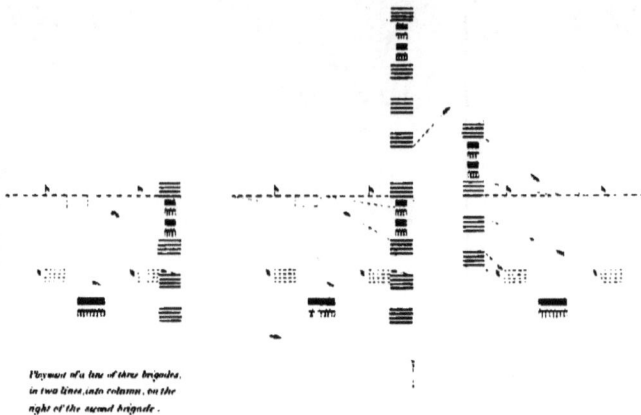

Ployment of a line of three brigades, in two lines, into column, on the right of the second brigade.
N°. 30.

33. If the brigade batteries are not in their respective columns, the distance between the leading subdivision of one brigade, and the rearmost subdivision of the brigade just in front of it, will be one hundred and fifty paces, whether the column be by company, or division, at half distance, or closed in mass.

34. If, however, the batteries are in the columns, the distance between the leading subdivision of one brigade, and the rearmost subdivision of the preceding brigade will be fifty paces, if the column is by company, and ninety paces, if the column is by division, and this, whether the column be at half distance, or closed in mass.

35. The major-generals will send staff officers in time, to mark the distance which should separate the brigades of their divisions when in column.

PART THIRD.

Article I.

To march in column at full distance.

Article II.

Column in route.

Article III.

To change direction in column at full distance.

Article IV.

To halt the column and to align it.

36. The movements prescribed in the above-named articles, will be executed according to the principles indicated Nos. 23 and 24.

37. If in column in route, the pieces of the batteries are not able, owing to the narrowness of the way, to march four abreast, the distance heretofore prescribed between brigades in column at full distance, will not be sufficient for the battery. A proper interval, however, for each battery must be obtained, and when the cadenced step is resumed, each battery will form as prescribed in the *E. B.*, No. 215, and the brigades will close up to their proper distances as prescribed No. 26.

Article V.

To close to half distance or in mass.

1st. To close the column on the leading subdivision.
2d. To close the column on the rearmost subdivision.
3d. To close the column on an interior brigade.

38. These movements will be executed according to the principles prescribed in the *E. B.*, and by the means indicated Nos. 23 and 24. The proper distances to be taken between brigades, are prescribed Nos. 33 and 34.

39. If necessary, the generals of brigade at the signal of *attention*, will with reference to their batteries, conform to what is prescribed in the *E. B.*, No. 145.

ARTICLE VI.

To march in column at half distance, or closed in mass.

ARTICLE VII.

To change direction in column at half distance.

ARTICLE VIII.

To change direction in column closed in mass.

1st. In marching.
2d. From a halt.

40. The movements prescribed by the above-named articles, will be executed according to the principles indicated Nos. 23 and 24.

41. In changing direction from a halt, each brigade after the leading one, will change direction by wheeling by its head out of the general column, and by being conducted by its brigadier-general to its new position in column.

ARTICLE IX.

Being in column at half distance, or closed in mass, to take distances.

1st. To take distances by the head of the column.

2d. *To take distances on the rear of the column.*
3d. *To take distances on the head of the column.*
4th. *To take distances on an interior column.*

42. The movements prescribed by the above-named articles, will be executed according to the principles indicated Nos. 23 and 24.

43. Prior to executing either of these movements however, the general will cause what is prescribed in the *E. B.*, No. 198, to be executed by each brigade of the column. After the distances are taken, the batteries will be ordered into the column by their respective generals of brigade, the colonels of the battalions having had care to leave for the batteries the proper intervals.

Article X.

Countermarch.

Article XI.

Being in column by company, to form divisions.

44. The movements prescribed by the above-named articles, will be executed according to the principles indicated Nos. 23 and 24.

PART FOURTH.

DIFFERENT MODES OF PASSING FROM THE ORDER IN COLUMN TO THE ORDER IN BATTLE.

ARTICLE I.

Manner of determining the line of battle.

45. The different modes of determining the line of battle have been explained in the E. B.

ARTICLE II.

Mode of passing from column at full distance into line of battle.

To the left (or *right*) *into line of battle.*

ARTICLE III.

Different modes of passing from column at half distance into line of battle.

1. *To the left (or right),*
2. *On the right (or left),*
3. *Forward by deployment,*
4. *Faced to the rear,*

} *into line of battle.*

ARTICLE IV.

Column closed in mass forward into line of battle.

Article V.

Formation into line of battle composed of two movements.

46. All the movements prescribed by the above-named articles will be executed according to the principles prescribed in the *E. B.*, and by the means indicated Nos. 23–4, the general having first determined the line of battle.

47. In the formation *forward*, or *faced to the rear* into line of battle, each brigade, other than the one of formation, will break by its head from the general column, and be conducted so that its leading battalion shall occupy its proper place in line. The brigadier-general will then deploy his brigade on the line as required.

48. In the successive formations in line, the general will send a staff officer to mark the point where the flank of each brigade which is nearest the one of formation ought to rest. *This rule is general, whether the battalions are to be deployed or remain in mass.*

REMARKS ON THE FORMATION IN LINE.

49. Habitually, the brigades will be formed on the line of battle in their proper order, viz.: *first, second, third, fourth, fifth, &c., &c.*

50. If, however, the general should deem it expedient to form line at once on the head of the column, and at the same time it is necessary to prolong the line both to the right and left, he **may** direct the brigades to be formed to the right

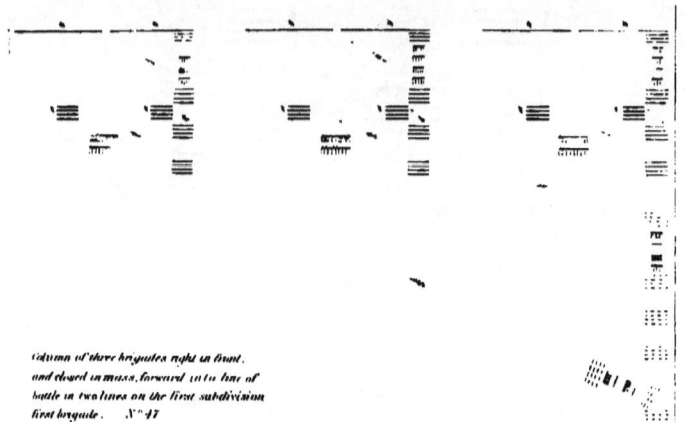

Column of three brigades right in front, and closed in mass, forward into line of battle in two lines on the first subdivision first brigade. Nº 47

and left of the *point d'appui*, without regard to the order of their numbers.

51. In this case, the brigades composing the divisions of the line being separated, the major-generals will be assigned commands temporarily by the general.

Article VI.

COLUMNS CLOSED IN MASS.

Deployment by battalion in mass.

52. A column in mass, whatever the number of brigades, may be formed into line of battle by deployment.
 1st. *Faced to the front.*
 2d. *Faced to the rear.*
 3d. *Faced to the left.*
 4th. *Faced to the right.*
 5th. *Oblique to the front*, or *rear*.

53. The general having determined the line of battle, the movements prescribed in the above-named article will be executed according to the principles indicated Nos. 23–4.

54. In the formations *faced to the front* or *rear*, each brigade, other than the one of formation, will break from the general column, as prescribed No. 47, and when the leading battalion has arrived on the line, the brigadier-general will complete its deployment.

55. In a line of battalions in mass, the distances between the brigades will habitually, in presence of the enemy, be such as to afford space for each brigade to deploy its masses, and to leave the

distance of one hundred and fifty paces between the flanks of the brigades.

56. If the line of masses constitute a part of the reserve, or other circumstances should render it expedient, the distances in line between the brigades can be reduced to fifty paces.

Movements which may be executed by a line of battalions in mass.

1st. *To advance in line.*
2d. *To halt the line marching in advance, and to align it.*
3d. *The line marching in advance, to cause it to change direction.*
4th. *To march the line in retreat.*
5th. *To change direction of the line marching in retreat.*
6th. *To break the line formed by battalion in mass into column.*
7th. *To ploy the line of masses into column.*
8th. *To take deploying intervals from a line formed by battalion in mass.*

57. The movements above prescribed, will be executed according to the principles indicated Nos. 23 and 24.

58. In ploying a line of masses into column, each brigade will ploy as if by itself, and it will then be conducted into the general column as indicated No. 31.

REMARKS ON INVERSION.

59. The principles prescribed in the *E. B.*,

No. 426 and following, for *breaking* or *ploying* into column a single brigade, are applicable to a line of many brigades.

PART FIFTH.

ARTICLE I.

To advance in line of battle deployed.

ARTICLE II.

To halt the line and to align it.

ARTICLE III.

Change of direction, marching in line of battle.

ARTICLE IV.

To retreat in line of battle.

ARTICLE V.

To halt the line marching in retreat, and to align it.

ARTICLE VI.

Change of direction marching in retreat.

Article VII.

March in line of battle of a line of brigades formed in battalion columns.

1st. To cause the line of columns to advance.
2d. To halt the line of columns and to deploy it.
3d. The line of columns marching in advance, to cause it to change direction.
4th. To cause line of columns to march in retreat.
5th. To halt the line of columns marching in retreat and to align it.
6th. The line of columns marching in retreat, to cause it to change direction.
7th. To close the intervals of a line of columns.

Article VIII.

March in line of battle by the flank of companies.

Article IX.

March in line of battle formed in division columns.

60. The movements prescribed in the above-named articles, will be executed according to the principles indicated Nos. 23 and 24.

61. In the alignment of deployed lines, the brigadier-general of that brigade on which the alignment is made, will not order his colors to their posts until the alignment is completed. The general will cause him to be notified of this fact.

62. In closing intervals, the general will cause the major-generals to be notified of the distance which should separate the brigades.

Article X.

To pass the defile in front.

Article XI.

To pass the defile in rear.

63. The movements prescribed by the above-named articles, will be executed according to the principles indicated Nos. 23 and 24.

64. In passing to the front, should the defile be opposite the interval between two brigades, all the subdivisions will wheel to the left or right, whether by platoon or company.

Article XII.

Changes of front.

Perpendicular changes of front.

1st. *Changes of front forward.*
2d. *Changes of front to the rear.*
3d. *Central changes of front.*

Oblique changes of front.

Article XIII.

ORDER IN ECHELON.

Direct echelons in advancing,

Direct echelons in retreat.

Oblique echelons.

Article XIV.

To retreat by alternate battalions.

To re-form the line.

Article XV.

Passage of line.

Article XVI.

Dispositions against cavalry.

Oblique squares.

To re-form the line.

65. The movements prescribed in the above-named articles, will be executed according to the principles indicated Nos. 23 and 24.

66. In retreating by alternate battalions, or in the passage of lines, the general of each line will cause the signal of *execution* to be sounded for the movement of his line.

67. In the passage of lines, if the general should not wish to pass the whole line at once, it will be executed by the second line of each brigade passing one at a time.

REMARKS ON THE FORMATION OF THE INFANTRY OF THE RESERVE.

68. When in-line, the infantry of the reserve should most generally be drawn up in close order, with the interval of twenty-two paces between the battalions in mass. In column, the distance between the brigades may be reduced to fifty paces.

Constitution of the reserve.

69. In a corps d'armée, the artillery of the reserve should be equal to one half the artillery of the line of battle.

70. The infantry of the reserve will be such part of the whole body as the general may think expedient, generally, however, it will be one-third.

71. The reserve will be under the especial direction of the general-in-chief.

72. The *special corps* including sappers, miners, pontoniers, &c., will be attached to the reserves, unless their services are otherwise needed.

73. The general may mass the whole or a portion of the brigade batteries, and cavalry forces, at one or several points on the field, as the state of the action, or his own judgment may suggest.

FINIS.

TABLE OF CONTENTS.

VOL. III.

TITLE VI.

EVOLUTIONS OF A BRIGADE.

	PAGE
General principles for the evolutions of a brigade (No. 1)	5
Posts of the brigadier-general in line and in column (No. 3)	5
General rules for commands (No. 7)	6
Position of the brigade battery (No. 17)	7
Position of the cavalry of the brigade (No. 20)	8

PART FIRST.

ARTICLE I.—To open and to close ranks (No. 21)............ 9
ARTICLE II.—Manual of arms (No. 25).................... 9
ARTICLE III.—Loading at will and the firings (No. 26). Remarks on firing (No. 45). To rest (No. 48). To stack arms (No. 52)... 10

PART SECOND.

ARTICLE I.—To break to the front, to the right or left into column (No. 58). To break to the right to march to the left (No. 63). Remarks (No. 67)....................... 15
ARTICLE II.—To break to the rear by the right or left into column (No. 68).. 17
ARTICLE III.—To ploy the line into close column or in mass, in rear of first division first battalion (No. 72). To ploy the line in rear or front of last division fourth battalion (No. 86). To ploy the line on first or last division of an interior battalion (No. 88). Remarks in ploying a line into a column closed in mass (No. 98)............. 19

PART THIRD.

ARTICLE I.—To march in column at full distance (No. 95).. 23
ARTICLE II.—Column in route (No. 103). Remarks (No. 108)... 25
ARTICLE III.—To change direction in column at full distance (109)... 26
ARTICLE IV.—To halt the column (No. 112). Remarks (No. 119)... 27
ARTICLE V.—To close the column or the leading company to half distance or in mass (No. 121). To close the column on the rearmost company (129). To close the column on an interior battalion (139). Remarks (No. 143)......... 28
ARTICLE VI.—To march in column at half distance or closed in mass (No. 146)... 33
ARTICLE VII.—To change direction in column at half distance (No. 150)... 34
ARTICLE VIII.—To change direction in column closed in mass in marching (No. 151). To change a direction from a halt (No. 155) 34
ARTICLE IX.—Being in column at half distance or closed in mass, to take distances by the head of column (No. 162). To take distances on the rear of the column (No. 166). To take distances on the head of the column (No. 178). To take distances on an interior battalion (No. 189.) Remarks on taking distances (No. 198)..................... 36
ARTICLE X.—Countermarch at full or half distance (No. 199). Countermarch of a column closed in mass (No. 204) 43
ARTICLE XI.—Being in column by company to form divisions (No. 208). Same on a march (No. 214). Remarks on the position of the battery in the column (No. 215). Position of the cavalry (No. 218)........................... 44

PART FOURTH.

ARTICLE I.—Manner of determining the line of battle (No. 219)... 46
ARTICLE II.—Mode of passing from column at full distance into line of battle (No. 220). By inversion to the right or left into line of battle (No. 225) Successive formations (No. 232)... 47
ARTICLE III.—Column at half distance to the left or right into line of battle (No. 237). Column at half distance on the right or left into line of battle (No. 240). Column at half distance forward into line of battle (No. 254). Remarks on forming forward into line of battle (No. 208).

CONTENTS.

	PAGE.
Column at half distance faced to the rear into line of battle (No. 271). To form into line faced to the rear without halting (No. 281)	58
ARTICLE IV.—Column closed in mass forward into line of battle or into line faced to the rear (No. 282)	59
ARTICLE V.—Formations into line of battle composed of two movements (No. 283)	60
ARTICLE VI.—Deployment by battalions in mass (No. 288). To deploy by battalion in mass, faced to the front, on first battalion (No. 289). Same movement without halting (No. 303). To deploy in mass on fourth battalion (No. 304). Line of battle on third, to deploy in mass on third battalion (No. 316). Line of battle on third to deploy in mass on the second battalion (No. 322). To deploy battalions in mass faced to the rear (No. 330). To deploy battalions in mass faced to the left (No. 331). To deploy by battalions in mass faced to the right (No. 338). To deploy by inversion faced to the right (No. 339). To deploy by battalions in mass, oblique to the front or rear (No. 344). Remarks on the movements of the battalions of the second line (No. 347). Remarks on the disposition of the brigade battery in formations from column into line (No. 348). To advance in line of battalions in mass (No. 350). To halt a line of battalions in mass, marching in advance and to align it (No. 362). The line marching in advance to cause it to change direction (No. 367). Remarks (No. 378). To march the line in retreat (No. 379). To change direction of the line marching in retreat (No. 388). To break the line formed by battalion in mass into column (No. 394). To ploy the line of masses into column (No. 399). The same movement in marching (No. 409). Remarks on forming a column closed in mass from a line of battalions in mass (No. 410). To take deploying intervals from a line formed by battalions in mass (No. 411). To take deploying intervals forward either parallel or oblique (No. 415). Remarks on disposition of companies of skirmishers in a line of battalions in mass (No. 425). Remarks on inversions (No. 426)	61

PART FIFTH.

ARTICLE I.—To advance in line of battle deployed (No. 430). General remarks on the march in line of battle (No. 457)	89
ARTICLE II.—To halt the line and to align it (No. 463)	96
ARTICLE III.—Change of direction marching in line of bat-	

	PAGE
tle (No. 474). Remarks on changes of direction marching in line of battle (No. 488)	93
ARTICLE IV.—To retreat in line of battle (No. 490)	101
ARTICLE V.—To halt the line marching in retreat, and to align it (No. 496)	102
ARTICLE VI.—Change of direction marching in retreat (No. 498)	103
ARTICLE VII.—March in line of battle of a line of battalions in columns (No. 507). To cause the line of columns to advance (No. 514). Remarks on the march of a line of battalion columns with deploying intervals (No. 534). To halt the line of columns and to deploy it (No. 538). The line of columns marching in advance to cause it to change direction (No. 546). To cause the line of columns to march in retreat (No. 554). To halt the line of columns marching in retreat and to align it (No. 558). The line of columns marching in retreat, to cause it to change direction (No. 560). To close the intervals of a line of columns (No. 565)	104
ARTICLE VIII.—March in line of battle of a line of deployed battalions by the flanks of companies (No. 573)	117
ARTICLE IX.—March in line of battle of a line of battalions formed in division columns (No. 575). Remarks on the disposition of the artillery with lines of battle (No. 577)	117
ARTICLE X.—To pass a defile in front (No. 578). Remarks on the passage of defiles in advancing (No. 595). Remarks on the disposition of the companies of skirmishers in passing a defile to the front (No. 600). Remarks on the passage of the defile in front by the second line (No. 602)	118
ARTICLE XL—To pass a defile in retreat (No. 603). Remarks on the disposition of the skirmishers in passing the defile in retreat (No. 615). Remark on the passing of the defile in retreat by the second line (No. 616). Remarks on the disposition of the artillery in passing defile in front or in retreat (No. 617)	124
ARTICLE XII.—Perpendicular change of front forward (No. 619). Change of front to the rear (No. 629). Central changes of front (No. 637). Oblique changes of front (No. 644.) Remark on changes of front (No. 647). Changes of front of two lines (No. 648)	123
ARTICLE XIII.—Order in echelon (No. 649). Direct echelons in advancing (No. 652). Direct echelons in retreat (No. 663). Oblique echelons (No. 671). Remarks on the order in echelons (No. 682)	134
ARTICLE XIV.—To retreat by alternate battalions (No. 688). To reform the line (No. 700). Remarks on the retreat by	

CONTENTS. 181

PAGE.
alternate battalions (No. 702). Remarks on the movements of the artillery in retreating by alternate battalions (No. 705).. 141
ARTICLE XV.—Passage of lines (No. 706). Remarks on the disposition of the artillery in the passage of lines (No. 717)... 145
ARTICLE XVI.—Dispositions against cavalry (No. 719). To form square echelons by battalions from column at half distance (No. 721). Same movement—the column at full distance (No. 727). Same movement—column closed in mass (No. 728). To form square when in column at half distance (No. 729). To form square when in column closed in mass (No. 731). To form square from line of battle (No. 734). Oblique squares (No. 740). To re-form the line (No. 746). Remark on oblique squares (No. 753). Remarks on the disposition of the artillery with the squares (No. 754).. 147

TITLE VII.

EVOLUTIONS OF A CORPS D'ARMEE.

General principles for the evolutions of a corps d'armée (No. 1)... 156
A division of the line (No. 2)........................... 156
Posts of the general-in-chief, of the major-generals, brigadier-generals, in line and in column (No. 4)............. 156
General rules for commands (No. 13).................... 158

PART FIRST.

ARTICLE I.—To open and close ranks.................... 160
ARTICLE II.—Loading at will and the firings............ 160
ARTICLE III.—To cause the line to rest................. 160

PART SECOND.

ARTICLE I.—To break to the front, to the right or left, into column.. 160
ARTICLE II.—To break to the rear by the right or left into column.. 162
ARTICLE III.—To ploy the line into column or in mass.... 162

PART THIRD.

ARTICLE I.—To march in column a full distance.......... 163
ARTICLE II.—Column in route........................... 163

VOL. III.—16.

ARTICLE III.—To change direction in column at full distance... 163
ARTICLE IV.—To halt the column and to align it.... 164
ARTICLE V.—To close to half distance or in mass.......... 164
ARTICLE VI.—To march in column at half distance or closed in mass 165
ARTICLE VII.—To change direction in column at half distance.... 165
ARTICLE VIII.—To change direction in column closed in mass.. 165
ARTICLE IX.—Being in column at half distance, or closed in mass, to take distances............................. 165
ARTICLE X.—Countermarch............................... 166
ARTICLE XI.—Being in column by company to form divisions 166

PART FOURTH.

ARTICLE I.—Manner of determining the line of battle...... 167
ARTICLE II.—Mode of passing from column at full distance into line of battle..................................... 167
ARTICLE III.—Different modes of passing from column at half distance into line of battle.................... 167
ARTICLE IV.—Column closed in mass formed into line of battle.. 167
ARTICLE V.—Formation into line of battle composed of two movements. Remarks on the formation in line........ 168
ARTICLE VI.—Deployment by battalion in mass. Movements which may be executed by a line of battalions in mass. Remarks on inversion............................ 169

PART FIFTH.

ARTICLE I.—To advance in line of battle, deployed........ 171
ARTICLE II.—To halt the line and to align it.............. 171
ARTICLE III.—Change of direction marching in line of battle 171
ARTICLE IV.—To retreat in line of battle................. 171
ARTICLE V.—To halt the line marching in retreat and to align it... 171
ARTICLE VI.—Change of direction marching in retreat.... 171
ARTICLE VII.—March in line of battle of a line of brigades formed in battalion columns......................... 172
ARTICLE VIII.—March in line of battle by the flank of companies.. 172
ARTICLE IX.—March in line of battle formed in division columns... 172

CONTENTS.

	PAGE.
ARTICLE X.—To pass the defile in front	173
ARTICLE XL—To pass the defile in rear	173
ARTICLE XII.—Changes of front	173
ARTICLE XIII.—Order in echelon	174
ARTICLE XIV.—To retreat by alternate battalions	174
ARTICLE XV.—Passage of lines	174
ARTICLE XVI.—Dispositions against cavalry	174
Remarks on the formation of the infantry of the reserve	175
Constitution of the reserve	175

www.ingramcontent.com/pod-product-compliance
Lightning Source LLC
Chambersburg PA
CBHW031741230426
43669CB00007B/436